THE MAVERICK

THE MAVERICK

MIMBRES PRESS
of Western New Mexico University

Interior Design by Jeremy Taylor: www.instagram.com/jeremy.taylor.ny

First Edition

Printed by Mimbres Press at Western New Mexico University.

ISBN (paperback): 978-1-958870-01-3 / (hardcover): 978-1-958870-00-6

mimbrespress.wnmu.edu

TABLE OF CONTENTS

Essays

Research

Meet the Editors

Yen Chu

Mimbres Press Advisory Board Member

Chief Editor of The Maverick

YEN CHU was born in Taichung, Taiwan, before her family immigrated to the U.S. As an East Asian, she learned to speak Mandarin Chinese at home and English at school, becoming fascinated with the dichotomy of Asian versus American culture. She immersed herself in the rich and colorful lifestyle of Silver City, New Mexico, studying the methods by which people may communicate and connect despite their differences. Now pursuing a BFA in Ceramics alongside a minor in Literature and Cell and Molecular Biology, she seeks to understand the networks that link people through the fine arts.

Katie DeLong
Editor

KATIE DELONG's major is in Interdisciplinary Studies and her concentrations are in English, Music, and Psychology. Once she completes her bachelor's degree, she plans to obtain an alternative licensure to become a teacher. Outside of academics, Katie enjoys honing her skills as a musician, playing video games, playing with her two cats, and spending time with friends and family.

Samantha Gonzales
Editor

SAMANTHA GONZALES is an aspiring teacher. She is majoring in Secondary Education with a focus in Fine Art. She is working towards completing her bachelor's degree and moving into working in a public school as a high school art teacher. She enjoys crafting and doing things such as crochet and beadwork. She loves spending time with her friends and cooking for them.

HEY, MUSTANGS!

Within the last year, the Mimbres Press of Western New Mexico University has gone from a concept to a real, active press. In half the time, our brand new undergraduate academic journal, *The Maverick*, has collected submissions to create and publish its very first online edition.

The Maverick owes its success to the hard work of its editors, as well as WNMU President Dr. Shepard, Valerie Plame, and their friends and colleagues for making the effort to bring the Mimbres Press and *The Maverick* to fruition. However, it owes its very core to our undergraduate Mustangs.

As a journal published by a university press, *The Maverick* is dedicated to the truthful representation of the WNMU student body. Our diversity, creativity, and innovation shine through in the following pages.

It is truly my pleasure to introduce this journal to you. I am honored to have been entrusted with its origination and to be able to present you with the work that will set a precedent for the future of our undergraduate press.

-YEN CHU

CREATIVE WRITING

Don't Blame Yourself, He Said to Me

Kelly Snyder

He was my best friend since I was 15.
His shit-eating grin was that of the Cheshire cats.
It was all you could see when he smiled at the world.
His eyes were so wide and bright,
You could see the stars dance in them by the moonlight.

We made each other laugh;
We were carefree and barefooted in the summer grass.
We would hold tight to each other when we were sad or scared.
As we grew older, the love we shared did not pass.
It grew grander with time,
Like the old oak tree we used to climb.

A few years would go by, here and there,
With no words to pass between us.
The phone would ring; it was like we had never been apart.
In the old days, I would twist the cord around my finger.
As times changed, we could catch that call in all places.
We would talk for hours about how our lives had been.

I can see his smile beaming through the phone,
The light of Gods shone upon me as we spoke.
As if we were the only two on Earth.

A few years back, I received one last call.
He told me of his platonic love for me, and I told of mine for him.
We have been through it all together.
Past loves, homelessness, and the woes of the world.
He seemed so happy, so alive, so in love with his wife and life.
She found him hanging from their front door.

His smile will never fade,
As bright as a supernova in the crisp night sky.
With his last thoughts, he wrote to me,
"Don't blame yourself; for now, I am free."
I wish to hear his smile,
Across the airwaves. Just one last time.

FEATURE

SPRING 2022
CREATIVE WRITING CONTEST

POETRY

FIRST PLACE

ATLANTIS LOPEZ is a senior at WNMU studying Elementary Teacher Education. She believes poetry is a unique art form that encompasses all human emotions and experiences.

Morning Serenity No Longer
ATLANTIS LOPEZ

Yesterday the rain fell upon the desert land
Misty morning serenity as Kabul awoke
Sun bright in the sky, radiant home of my heart

I wonder when the rain turned into a river of tears and blood
The children who used to play with kites
Soaring above the souks, now lie
Asleep in the river, eyes closed forever

Today, the English sea, a dark opaque kind of blue is angry
Waves lapping violently on the shore
It reminds me of the water I had to cross
Unkind and cruel, swallowing those who fell off the makeshift boat

I come to the sea to listen for an answer
To know if the world will stay broken, if it always was?
But it doesn't talk to me, at least not of what I want to hear or remember
It makes me think of things from a past life

Of morning serenity, Kabul sun rising
The home that is no longer mine
Thanks to the song of war, a sad melody of destruction
A song no one should ever hear

I am a refugee
Now I will always wander
Heart reaching back to what once was

I can remember his eyes when I close mine
As black as obsidian stone
The kind that pierced your soul
In the camps, I would ask if they'd seen him
"He has black eyes and black hair." I would say
Sounds like every little boy here they would say
But that was me pretending he was still here

He's not like every other boy,
His eyes are as black as the night
When the light touches them just right
They turn to glass

His eyes were glass when the explosion took him

I wish I could forget his eyes
In their permanent state of glass
And forget the blood, the tears, the screams
I wish I didn't have to close his eyes
"My beautiful boy,
Cause of death, this broken world."
Playing on the floor with legos
He's building a big house
He looks up at me with those eyes
Those piercing eyes and asks
"Do the houses break in England like they do here?"
Holding back tears I say no

The trouble is houses break everywhere
Some in worse shape than others
Broken by bombs, guns, drugs, or lack of love

I'm glad he is not here in this foreign English land
He would not like it
He is a child of the desert
Like father, like son
His heart will always stay buried
In the sand of our homeland
Running along the banks of the mighty river
Kicking the dust of Afghanistan behind him
Feeling the warmth of a thousand splendid suns
Rising over Kabul in perfect radiance
Turning his eyes into glass
In permanent serenity

SECOND PLACE

NAYELI MANCILLA is a freshman student athlete from Phoenix, Arizona. She plays on the Western New Mexico Women's Volleyball team and plans on majoring in Art Education.

Anxiety
NAYELI MANCILLA

Debilitating, vicious
impatient, and unkind.
No one said to lay in bed
grim thoughts won't leave my mind.
Heartbeat racing, isolating
sleepless nights consume.
No matter how it won't stop now,
don't want to leave this room.

Afraid to fail, to no avail
you see me as a try.
To lead them all, let no one fall
behind so they don't cry.

Overthinking while I'm sinking
hard work is what you see.
Unease and doubt won't help me out
I send a silent plea.

Reoccurring, vision blurring
fear beats my inner peace.
Can't say no, afraid to show
the head of this disease.

Eager to please, fall to my knees
in the privy of my home.
Perception and perfection are
the reason I'm alone.

Anxiety, society,
what a dire blend.
The two can only disagree
the mind simply cannot bend.

Chest is tight, nothing's right
the room begins to spin.
I find my breath and count to three
and search for strength within.

Quality of presence,
quietness of peace.
My body's fine, my mind is numb,
negativity deceased.

Time passes slow, although I know,
these feelings dissipate.
A place inside myself I find
I can appreciate.

PROSE / PLAYS

FIRST PLACE

NADIEN CHAVEZ moved to New Mexico about four years ago to be closer to family. She currently works as a licensed practical nurse in Las Cruces, New Mexico, transitioning to the education field. She is the first one in her family to earn a college degree. Her current hobbies include taking care of her plants, walking her dog, and exploring New Mexico. She is scheduled to graduate in Spring 2023 with her bachelor's degree in secondary education.

The Intruder
One-Act Play for Two People
NADIEN CHAVEZ

[On a cold and dark fall evening in a rural neighborhood outside of town is a large well-lit home.]

Lily (excited):
Bye Mom, bye Dad! Have a fun night, love you!

Sarah (smiling):
Have a good evening, Mr. and Mrs. Lopez. I promise I'll take good care of Lily.
[Both girls stand waving at Lily's parents from the doorway.]

Sarah (quickly turning to Lily):
Ok Lily, here is the plan. I am going to be in the spare room on the phone and you can stay here in the living room.

Lily (nervously asks):
Uh, why aren't you going to hang out with me?

Sarah:
I will later, but I really need to talk to my best friend. She needs me.

Lily:

But . . . I-I-I wanted to hang out with you. And- I really don't like being all by myself.

Sarah:

You will be fine, don't worry. I am in the room right next door.

Lily (pleading):

Please Sarah. Please, please, please hang out with me. I don't like being alone by myself.

Sarah (taking a deep breath) while texting on her phone:

Lily . . . you are eleven years old. It's time for you to grow up a little bit.

Just call me if you need anything. Please?

[Sarah exits to the bedroom off to the right. Lily sits down on the sofa and begins painting her nails while the TV plays in the background.]

Side Bedroom:

[Sarah laying belly down on the bed, feet crossed and up in the air, talking on the phone. Her laughter fills the house. Lily remains in the living room.]

Sarah (excitedly talking on the phone with her friend):

No way! Shut up! Uh huh….

Yeah. And what did he say?

Are you serious??

(Gasps) O-M-G! I can't believe you told him that.

[Tap, tap, tap on the living room window.]

[Sarah stops talking.]

Hold on! (Whispers abruptly to her friend on the phone.)

[Sarah curiously looking around the room.

The phone remains on her ear.]

Wait, Jen . . . stop talking.

[Pause]

Yes, I am fine. I thought I heard something.

Sarah (sounding concerned) calls out to Lily:

Lily?

[No response.]

[Sarah shrugs her shoulders and resumes her call.]

Whatever. She must be playing with her little dolls or something.

Sarah giggles (talking on the phone):

No way! I am not going to check. Why? Ummm . . . Maybe because I am busy talking to you.

No, Lily will be fine. Whatever. OK, so what were we talking about? [laughing continues]

Living room:

[The muffled sound of the TV is heard in background. Lily is oblivious to the first sound.]

[Tap, tap, tap. Now, on the back kitchen window.]

Lily jumps up and runs to the spare room shouting:

Sarah! Sarah! Sarah!

[Sarah quickly opens the bedroom door.]

Sarah (frantically):

What?! What is it? Are you ok?

Lily:

I–I–I heard a sound. This thing!

[Pointing to the back window.]

Sarah (casually):

Oh Lily, I remember when I was your age, I

was afraid of everything.

Lily (eagerly) while pulling on Sarah's sweater:

Please, Sarah. I'm scared.

Sarah (reluctantly):

Fine, Lily. You are so annoying sometimes. I'll check it out.

[Rolling her eyes.]

[Sarah carelessly looks out the back kitchen window. Just as she is about to walk away, something caught her eye.]

Lily (noticing Sarah's demeanor):

Wh-wh-what do you see?

Sarah (shakes her head):

Uh-Um . . . nothing. It was a cat. Only a cat. Let's get back to enjoying our night.

Lily (scared):

Are you sure, Sarah? Because I'm pretty sure I heard something.

Sarah (hands on her hips/confidently):

Lily, I promise you, I didn't see anything. I know what I saw. And it was a cat.

Lily:

But–but–I swear . . .

Sarah (apathetically):

Enough! You swear nothing. I'll order pizza soon. Happy?

[Sarah exits the stage to the spare bedroom. Lily sits on the sofa in the living room.]

Lily (aside to the audience):

I wish Sarah understood why I don't like being left alone. A few years ago my brother died while home alone during an earthquake. I don't like thinking about it.

Side Bedroom:

[Sitting at the edge of the bed, Sarah finds herself in a daze.]

Sarah (aside to the audience):

I'm not crazy right? It was a cat.

[Sarah resumes her call with her friend.]

[While in the living room . . . an abrupt interruption on the TV startles Lily. The broadcaster warns "Neighborhood intruder on the loose. Lock your doors."]

Lily (shouting):

Sarah!!!!

[Lily bangs on the bedroom door. Thump, thump, thump.]

Sarah quickly opens the bedroom door (annoyed tone):

What now, Lily?

Lily (scared):

Sarah! You won't believe it. The man on the TV said there is an intruder in our area.

Sarah (reassuringly):

Yeah, right. Even if there was an intruder, I'll protect us. Plus, who knows where he's at?

Lily:

What if he comes here? What do we do?

Sarah (softly chuckles):

Seriously? I doubt he will come here.

[a few seconds of silence pass.]

[The boom of thunder sounds outside along with the pattering of rain.

Knock, Knock, knock at the front door.]

Lily (scared):

Uh, who's that?

Sarah (whispers):

I-I-I am not sure.

Lily (whispers):
Go check.

Sarah:
No, you go check.

Lily (whispering and attempts to reach for Sarah's hand for comfort):
You are the babysitter, go check.

[Sarah tiptoes to the front door and looks through the peep hole. There's nothing.]

Sarah (suspiciously):
That's weird . . . there is no one there.

Lily:
I don't like this, Sarah. Should we call the police?

Sarah:
No, no . . . uh-uh-ummm . . .

Sarah (puts on a fake smile and attempts to distract Lily):
Everything is fine. We are fine. Do you want to play a board game?

Lily:
Uh . . . I guess. But what about the—

Sarah (cuts Lily off):
No. No what about anything. Okay? We are fine. Let's just focus on having fun.

[Suddenly, a loud bang at the back kitchen door. The door unexpectedly swings open.]

[The girls jump back, and grab hold of one another. The dark figure of a man is now in the doorway.]

Sarah (shouts):
Run, Lily!

[Both girls run into spare room off to the side of the living room. The door slams shut behind them. Hugging each other out of fear for their lives, they are breathing heavily and shaking.]

Lily (quietly begins to cry):
I told you Sarah. I told you I heard something, and you didn't believe me.

Sarah (whispering and soothing tone):
Shhhh . . . or he will hear us.

[One to two minutes pass.]

Sarah (whispering and putting a finger up to her lips in a quiet motion):
Stay here and don't make a sound.

Lily (whispering):
Where are you going?

Sarah (whispering):
Shhh . . . I said stay here. I'll be right back.

[Sarah places her ear up to the bedroom door. She hears nothing.]

Sarah (whispers to Lily):
Stay under the bed. Use my cell phone to call 911. Tell them what's happening.

Lily (sniffling):
Ok. Where are you going? I want my mom and dad.

Sarah:
I think he left. I just heard the back door shut. I'll be right back, I promise.

[She smiles at Lily.]

[Sarah tiptoes into the living room quietly.]

Suddenly, Sarah shouts:
Lily! Help me! Call the police!

[Sounds of shattered glass and thumps on the furniture filled the house. A struggle was taking place in the living room.]

Lily [aside to the audience]:

It's time to be brave and face my fears. No matter what happens.

[Lily takes a deep breath, grabs a bat, and runs out to the living room to help Sarah.]

[With all her strength, Lily pulls the bat back and swings at the mystery figure with all her strength.]

[A brief rumble ensues until it stops.]

[Standing over the figure, both girls are sweating, out of breath, and frightened.]

[Red and blue lights begin flashing outside the living room.

Both girls begin to cry.]

Sarah:

Is he dead? Did we kill him?

Lily (breathing heavily):

I can't believe we got him. I-I-I don't know what took over me.

Sarah (hugs Lily tightly):

Thank you, Lily, for being so brave and saving us.

[(Swoosh), the front door swings open.]

[To Lily's relief, her parents come running in alongside the police.]

The End

SECOND PLACE

ASHLEI R. GARCIA is an undergraduate student at Western New Mexico University who is exploring education as her major, as well as other interdisciplinary work. She was born and raised right here in Silver City, New Mexico, where she is raising her two children with her husband. Her family's deep historical roots to the region, her Mexican heritage, and Latinx identity influenced her essay showcased in the Creative Writing contest.

Southwest Granny
ASHLEI R. GARCIA

My grandma has always been the heart and soul of the family. She has always been someone to look up to, brave, and never afraid. She was a nurse, so she knows what real patience and nurturing is about. I can describe her as someone who has been through a lot of historical events and somewhat inventions. The main thing I loved about her was her outspoken and brutally honest voice. She wasn't afraid to say how she felt. In the late '90s on Kelly Street in historic downtown Silver City, I'd play on this cement rock wall and pick apricots from a tree in my grandma's backyard. The cicadas would chirp in the blazing southwest summer day that would be cooled down by the afternoon monsoons. She'd sit on the porch smoking Pall Mall reds and drink her coffee from her signature white mug while we played.

I was always with my grandma because my mom was a single mother of three and worked a full-time job. So, she got me prepared for my next stage of life which was school. I was 5 years old, and August rolled around the corner quick. That whole summer, I was dreading it to be over only because I didn't want to go to school. I was so nervous only because I've not once been away from her. As we're walking into the elementary, all I could focus on was the florescent lights and the smell of new school supplies and freshly waxed floors.

As we get closer to the classroom, I grab her hand tighter and she looks down at me and says, "It's going to be ok." I didn't want to go; the separation anxiety was setting in full force. She then let my hand go as the teacher was welcoming me. I couldn't hold it any longer. I started crying hysterically. She walked away with tears in her eyes. The day went on and all I could think about was being at her house; the smell of coffee and cigarettes was somewhat a safe haven for me. The school day was over and as we are walking in line to be released, I see her standing on her porch waving at me (she lived across the street of the school) and at that moment I knew that was my "home" my grandma.

As I got older, she had always been someone I looked up to only because she wasn't afraid of anything. She always had a strong mindset, I thought she was invincible. She was a nurse who worked at all the historic hospitals: Fort Bayard, it's now demolished; the Hillcrest, which was demolished and rebuilt into a senior citizen apartment complex that overlooks Silver City. After she retired, she became a caregiver of the elderly as well as the "family nurse." Anything we thought was wrong physically we didn't go to the doctor's office or the hospital, we simply called Grandma Lee. Both of my pregnancies I would be there asking her questions from A to Z and she always had the right answer for me.

We didn't see her as just a grandma or a nurse but as a walking history book. She was born in 1931, so she had been through a lot of events and inventions that occurred in history. My brothers and I would always ask her questions about "back in the day" because she was alive when Hitler was doing the evil things he was doing. She lived through presidential assassinations, when Pearl Harbor got bombed, when bathrooms weren't built into the houses. And the start of a lot of wars. For example, she would explain to us how she had to go outside to an outhouse to use the bathroom.

She, her brothers, and sister would be scared to go at night because of the darkness and noises. She hated it when it was cold too. If you wanted to know anything from that time frame from a first person, she would be the person to go to. It's so amazing that I can say I knew someone who lived through all that. Everyone loved my grandma for not only her compassion but her brutal honesty to her outspoken voice. She told you how it was and if you didn't like it then oh well, she said what she said. She didn't see anything wrong with it. I was heavily pregnant with my second son and walked into her house on a hot summer day. She looks at me and says, "you look pitiful" with no remorse or a care. Just blunt and to the point. I didn't know how to react to that. But she called it how it was and that is exactly how I felt. I'm shy and timid. My grandma taught me how to be out of my shell and express my voice, or you will never be heard. Like in high school I was terrified to get up and do presentations. I couldn't figure out how to overcome it so I usually would take the zero for the assignment. If I knew what she meant, then I would have done so much better. So now being a college freshman, 13 years out of high school, when I get called on to answer a question and I hear my grandma's voice telling me to speak. I love her for that.

It wasn't until her later years that she developed emphysema, due to her smoking her whole life. The doctors told her she would have to quit and get put on oxygen. She was spiteful and resentful towards it but she dealt with it. In 2013, we got the most gut-wrenching news that my Aunt Sherry passed away from colon cancer. It took a big toll on my grandma's health. Not long after that, we found out my grandma had lung cancer. My whole insides shattered. She didn't want treatment. She wanted to die happy. She started deteriorating rapidly. Then she had a bad fall and broke her hip she just had replaced.

The strong invincible grandma I once knew was leaving me. She became hospitalized then got sent home under hospice care. My grandma passed away five days after my first son's birthday. Two days before my mother's birthday. As she laid in her bed slowly dying, I grabbed her hand with it just being us two in the room. All my memories with this woman came flashing through my mind. All the years we spent together. Everything she ever showed me. Taught me. I told her "Thank you for teaching me everything I know. I love you my grandma." Broken and in disbelief, I kissed her on the head and let her hand go, knowing I will never speak to her again. A piece of my heart left with her as she moved on to the afterlife. I will always and forever love my grandma. My true hero.

ART

ASHLEY COOVER

Before wedging a new mound of clay, there is an idea that has been brewing in my thoughts. This thought weaves in and out of my conscious and subconscious like a flag fluttering in the distance, surrendering to the playfulness and chaos of a passing breeze. You notice it, focus on the thing, but cannot quite put your finger on what it is that is holding your attention captive. It is in these moments of awe that I absorb inspiration.

When the notion begins to morph into adjectives, feelings, or symbols, I can only hope my recollection of this idea's impression will be conceived accurately through the balance of my skills and abilities. Always starting a new work with high ideals and expectations, my process begins.

While I am developing my craft and artistic voice at Western New Mexico University, I am enjoying my exploration of atmospheric kilns. The ceramics department is built upon pillars of investigation and research. From my studies, I have come to favor a good stoneware sturdy enough for handbuilding but soft enough to throw, and light in color. The light-colored clay body plays the role of a canvas to surface designs that include gestural applications of layered glazes. Currently, my work thrives across the spectrum of sculpture and utilitarian vessels. In my time remaining at WNMU, I hope to have a narrower scope in my portfolio and plan to exhibit internationally.

ISMELDA GARZA

Sunday Mass

New WNMU Program:
Ceramics
Post- Baccalaureate

SUSIE MESKILL

Susie is a ceramic artist currently living in Silver City. She moved here from Colorado last August and is originally from St. Louis, Missouri. She moved out west for college to spend more time in nature and explore the Rocky Mountains. She has always enjoyed creating with her hands, whether it be a quilt, jewelry, or ceramic objects. In the last five years, her ceramic pursuit has become more serious after being an apprentice to a Denver-based potter. She accepted the position as post-bacc at WNMU to have more support in furthering her education in clay and in developing her style and techniques.

HOW DID ART AND CERAMICS BECOME A PART OF YOUR LIFE? WHAT MADE YOU DECIDE TO PURSUE IT AS A CAREER?

I have always loved making and building things. In high school, I took my first pottery class at a community studio in St. Louis and loved it right away. I loved the feeling of using my hands to make a tangible object and getting to personalize it during the entire process. When I went to college, I studied psychology and put my interest in clay on the back burner. I didn't know I could actually pursue it as a career. It wasn't until I met a local potter (Jessa Decker-Smith) who made a living from selling her work in the community, teaching classes at elementary schools, and occasionally giving private lessons, that I realized it could be a career path. She generously let me work out of her studio for a while and then hired me to help teach after-school classes. I soon had several unexpected opportunities pop up, like having a booth at a maker's market, selling mugs at local coffee shops, and being commissioned to make cups for a popular bakery. I was inspired by Jessa to host my own backyard sales and the turnout was incredible. I started to gain confidence in my work and wanted to dedicate more time and energy into pursuing ceramics as my career.

WHAT KIND OF EXPERIENCE HAVE YOU HAD AT WNMU SO FAR?

At the beginning of 2021, I started looking for ceramic opportunities online. I was mainly looking at apprenticeships around the country because I wanted a way to learn more in a supportive setting. After working out of my home studio for the majority of the pandemic, I found myself stuck making the same types of mugs and bowls over and over again. I didn't even really know what a post-bacc program was until I read about the one at WNMU on the Ceramic Arts Network website. There was a posting for a year-long position that offered mentorship and studio space in exchange for technical help around the studio each week. I put together a portfolio and artist statement and applied in April.

I really had no clue what to expect from the program and had never been to Silver City before moving here. I hoped there would be a fun, tight-knit ceramics community at WNMU, and that has definitely been the case.

Since I've come to Western, the way I view and understand art has changed completely. I've been exposed to more ceramic art than ever before. I've been inspired by nature, architecture, furniture, and design from the past century. I love seeing patterns in all of these elements and trying to incorporate that into my new pieces. The fun begins as I try to understand why I am so drawn to certain forms, colors, and surface texture. I am starting to notice what feelings and concepts I want my work to express and that feels like an entirely different process from making mugs out of my garage a couple of years ago.

WHAT SHOULD A NEW POST-BACC CANDIDATE KNOW OR EXPECT?

I would say that they should go for it if they are trying to understand what a career as a ceramic artist could look like and if they want to develop their techniques in the studio. The post-bacc program gives you space to work on your own projects with all the materials you could ever need. However, it definitely takes a lot of self-accountability and time management skills to be able to know how to prioritize time in and outside of the studio. This program provides the opportunity to experiment in the studio as much as possible. My favorite part has been making things that I never could have imagined making a year ago.

Courtney Michaud, the ceramics professor here at WNMU, has been such an incredible mentor and helped make the move as seamless as possible. There was a big learning curve in going from making ceramics out of my house to having access to an entire studio of endless clay and glaze materials. It's opened my mind to what I can create and how to look at my work through a more artistic perspective, and it's been awesome to be surrounded by other people going through the exact same process. I've loved meeting people in the studio and then bumping into them in the grocery store or seeing them on the trails near campus. Silver is such a unique place and is unlike anywhere else I've ever lived.

33

ESSAYS

Bullying: The United States' Own Epidemic

Atziry N. Jordan

School bullies have seemingly always had a place in the circle of life that has existed in our education system. Today, bullying has been taken much more seriously on account of students who are bullied or cyberbullied are twice as likely to commit suicide or have suicidal ideations (Hinduja & Patchin, 2018). Social media platforms have opened Pandora's box to a newer, ever-evolving way of bullying and harassment. Phones can be confiscated in class, but words and thoughts linger long after class has been dismissed and present themselves in the form of a "snap" or "tweet," attacking or humiliating an individual for the school, community, and internet to see. Anti-bullying statements make nice posters and newsletters, but social media has created an entirely unique environment that is much more difficult to control. Students face many social issues while pursuing their education. Some will undoubtedly face bullying for disabilities, poverty, scrutiny of sexual preference or gender identity and racism, abuse, neglect, and 21% of these students, which equates to 5 million, will have to endure the abuse of bullying within the education system (Hinduja & Patchin, 2018).

As the individual who was depicted as a whale on the white board while my history teacher scoffed and read his sports section of the newspaper is a memory stained with self-hate, disgust, and has caused a trickle effect of eating disorders, self-image problems and at one point, suicidal ideations in my life. The teacher failed me, and society has failed its children by allowing "harmless banter" and "locker-room talk" to fester into a monster capable of taking any form it chooses. The bottom line remains that despite the circumstances a student faces in their personal lives, they should be granted the opportunity to earn and enjoy their education without fear of persecution or harassment.

THE EVOLUTION OF THE BULLY

Bullies have been depicted throughout the decades in a common way: the bigger, more popular, or even more athletic individual with a knack for picking on the "little guy" and the beautiful, essentially perfect prom queen singling out the "nerdy girl." The traditional physical bullying we as society often assume is the bullying still in effect, is only one of four types of bullying. Gale (2019) describes four categories of bullying that have been named by advocates against bullying. These categories are physical, verbal, social or emotional bullying, and cyberbullying. Physical and verbal bullying remain forms of bullying that can be minimized and apprehended within the school system and in classrooms. Social or emotional bullying, along with cyberbullying, creates the new frontier of bullying. Social bullying aims to denigrate a student's social standing amongst peers through rumors or exclusion (Gale, 2019). The isolating and sort of "classing" that occurs within the schools is not a new idea, however; it is a well understood design flaw built into the pillars of the public education system. Inglis explains what he deems as the true purpose behind the modern school systems, stating "Schools are meant to tag the unfit—with poor grades, remedial placement, and other punishments—clearly enough that their peers will accept them as inferior and effectively bar them from the reproductive sweepstakes that's what all those little humiliations from first grade onward were intended to do, wash the dirt down the drain" (Gatto, 2008, p. 139). Further, the division and isolation of students from lesser means is thought of as a "trained" behavior, according to Gatto (2008) who says, "Divide children by subject, by age-grading, by constant rankings on tests, and many other more subtle means, and it was unlikely that the ignorant mass of mankind, separated in childhood, would ever reintegrate into a dangerous whole" (p. 138).

CYBERBULLYING

Cyberbullying is the newest representation of bullying, utilizing virtually every platform that the internet offers to anonymously bully and victimize unsuspecting individuals at the click of a button. Social media, instant messaging, chatrooms, blogs, and mobile phone applications like Facebook, Snapchat, Twitter, TikTok, and Instagram now exist at the fingertips of children, adolescents, and yes, even scorned adults to misuse at their will. According to the U.S. Department of Health and Services, CDC (Centers for Disease Control) (2018), 14.9% of students across the U.S. reported bullying through electronic means. Even if 14.9% of the student population nationwide does not appear as a large statistic, the alarming factor that remains is that this percentage of the student population is twice as likely to self-harm or have suicidal ideations (John et al., 2018). With adolescents already being vulnerable to self-esteem issues, the percent of students who did report cyberbullying, while the number may truly be much higher, is cause for concern to educators, legislators, parents, and administrators alike. Students who have been targets for cyberbullying can often feel silenced by the overwhelming presence social media and the internet present in their lives. While skipping school intentionally can be considered truant behavior, 10% of students who do not feel safe at school report skipping at least one day to avoid their bullies and 60% of all U.S.

students report noticing a significant hinderance on their ability to learn or feel safe in school if they are being bullied (Hinduja, 2018). Cyberbullying plays a significant role in students' inability to truly pursue their education and is a growing aspect of bullying which has little rules or laws now that could cause an effective sort of cease and desist.

Discriminatory Bullying

Discrimination is neither a new issue to the United States' education system nor is it a matter that can truly be abolished anytime soon; it can, however, be acknowledged, and the proper measures can be taken to lessen the severity of its impact on students. There are several different influences on a student's vulnerabilities in their respected education institution and most of them are utterly out of the control of the victim, especially if the bullying is about their appearance, cultural background, or self-identity. Statistically, 135,200 student allegations of bullying stemming from discrimination were reported in the 2015-16 academic year (U.S. Department of Education & OCR, 2019). The fact behind this statistic and many like it represents that students are being disproportionately affected by bullying and it is having a direct impact on their willingness to pursue their education. According to the NCES (2016), students who experience bullying based on several different aspects have larger fears of physical harm, experience deteriorating mental, physical, and academic well-being along with avoiding school altogether. The differing factors that can accost to students being bullied include learning and mental disabilities, the LGBTQ+ community, students struggling with gender identity, students who live in poverty or face homelessness, and racism along with cultural beliefs or practices.

The belief that these students are somehow "less than" their peers based on these factors is not only degrading but harmful to the generations of students who already struggle with their places in society.

Disabilities

Students who believe they have been victimized due to their disabilities accounted for 11% of the before-mentioned 135,200 students who reported instances of bullying (U.S. Department of Education & OCR, 2019). These students may face bullying in the classroom or in social situations like gym class and sports. When students who are already facing disadvantages in the manner they can receive their education become the targets of bullying, it not only discourages them from their education but also presents a new danger of mental health issues like depression and anxiety. Students with disabilities are already presented with difficulties succeeding in their education like facing standardized tests and a curriculum regulated to the whole student body rather than an individualized approach. Special Education students even report that they feel more physical, emotional, and psychological distress as a direct result from bullying, along with a higher rate of teachers or staff being the perpetrators (Hartley, Bauman, Nicon & Davis, 2015). Students with physical disabilities can become easier targets of physical bullying due to a minimized ability to defend themselves. Students who suffer from learning disabilities, emotional and behavior disorders, or those with other similar disorders also report higher rates of experiencing bullying than their peers (Rose & Gage, 2017). Instances where individuals with disabilities feel disproportionately victimized due to circumstances far outside anyone's control are troubling, yet they happen at a much more frequent rate than perhaps the education system would like to recognize.

LGBTQ+

Students identifying within the LGBTQ+ community experience harassment and high rates of teacher reporting failure (Kosciw, et al., 2018). Middle school and high school youth who consider themselves to belong in the LGBTQ+ community also feel unsafe and uncomfortable due to their sexual orientations, reporting these concerns at a staggering 61% of the student population (CDC, 2017). A few decades ago, it would have been relatively unheard of for students to "come out" as members of the LGBTQ+ community in the way they are able to now, but a societal acceptance of their identity does not guarantee them safety in their own classrooms and schools. In 2015, a survey of LGBTQ+ youth from the ages 13-21 revealed that: 10% had been harmed or threatened with weapons, 18% had experienced dating violence, and 18% of these students had been sexually assaulted (CDC, 2017). If the math is done correctly, 1,260 students had not only been abused in relationships, but had also been sexually assaulted due to their sexual orientation. These students are harassed in every aspect of their school life, peers have prejudices against them, stereotypes set them up as easy and unintimidating targets, and experiencing teacher reporting failure are all instances enough to see why these students' last priority is their education; they are preoccupied with maintaining their safety. It is not a shock to learn that the LGBTQ+ youth who experience rejection at home and at school are eight times more likely to attempt suicide and six times as likely to have higher levels of depression (CDC, 2017).

POVERTY

When a student's financial status is brought into question, it is not assumed that it would have any real bearing on a student's level of harassment. This assumption is wrong for a few reasons. While the general student population may not seem to take notice of a student's financial background, often it is the first quality used to assess whether an individual is worthy of friendship or if they can be disregarded like the "trash" they come from. It is a harsh statement to make, of course, but not as harsh as the actual treatment and derogatory slander a student with a "poor" life will endure. Making matters worse, students who come from impoverished families or backgrounds are more likely to act out as bullies, whether it be a defense mechanism or sheer aggression channeled into a negative form. According to Gertsl-Pipen (2005), these negative behaviors become prevalent in a classroom and are associated with a student's insecurities (p. 152). Staff are key to identifying behavioral problems and helping stop it before it becomes an aggravated situation: "Assessments helped us identify students who were most in need of attention. What we found is that our students are really good at looking good, even if they don't understand" (Gertsl-Pipen, 2005, p. 152).

COVID-19

In times of COVID-19, students' home lives have been thrust into light for all a student's peers and educators to see. While some students may enjoy giving personal tours into the home that they have virtually been confined to for the duration of the pandemic, students from low-income housing or circumstances might dread the occasion. School closures meant remote learning, which indicates a student should have an internet connection and a laptop with video capabilities.

To the students who did not possess these means and the school systems who had delayed responses to these circumstances, it means a disadvantaged student and another learning delay placed in their paths. One author's opinion is that schools closing will have long-lasting effects from this pandemic, stating that "The fact that schools are closed for a long period of time could have detrimental social and health consequences for children living in poverty and are likely to exacerbate existing inequalities" (Van Lancker, 2020). The impact of COVID-19 not only presents educational challenges but the vulnerability of isolation and bullying to students from low-income households. These students will experience "long-lasting consequences for children's health, well-being, and learning outcomes" (Van Lancker, 2020).

Racism and cultural differences are also not new representations to the dynamic that leads to student bullying or targeting, but when the education systems attempt to shift blame from poverty or underfunding, they often credit students of color as the underlying issues within the school system (Gerstl-Pepin, 2005, p. 148). When former President George W. Bush's administration implemented the "No Child Left Behind" act to improve the American education system, the administration took credit for higher testing grades and standards than they had been before. Bush would, however, loosely use the terms "inner city" in a manner that blamed failure to succeed on low-income minority students, pushing the idea that lower-class students are the proprietors of low test scores (Gerstl-Pepin, 2005, p 148). By blaming students of color for failure of success in the school system, students of color can become targets for blame, which is not theirs at all. Many students of color have turned to homeschooling as an alternative to avoiding or reducing the bullying and targeting that can occur. Of the homeschooled students' numbers, minority students made up 32% in 2012 (Ray, 2017, p. 608). When parents were asked to indicate their important reasoning for homeschooling their students, the top answer was "concerned about other schools' environments, desire to provide religious instruction, and dissatisfaction with academic standards" (Ray, 2017, p. 609). According to Ray (2017), when asked the reasons why African-American parents chose to homeschool their children, 40% of the parents stated they wanted to homeschool their children to provide them with more education on American Black culture and history (p. 609). Furthermore, 20% of the parents directly stated that "they desire to avoid racism in public schools" (Ray, 2017, p. 609). Research greatly suggests that minorities have homeschooled their children for fear of exposure to things like "racism, violence, drugs, etc.," (Ray, 2017, p 609).

HIGH TEST SCORES, LOW BULLYING RATE: COINCIDENCE?

While it seems like a bleak circumstance presented by the ever-evolving cases of bullying, hope presents itself for students and educators looking to halt this unfortunate occurrence. One elementary school in particular, Maple Elementary School, has been noted as doing much more than only improving the testing environment and scores of its students. Maple Elementary, led by Dr. Jordon, is breaking the educational molds that are often responsible for the failure to prevent or redirect bullies and victims' attentions from their social circumstances back to their education. The approach Maple Elementary educators take to ensure every student's well-being is supported by their code, one of the main focuses being "Every child is important at Maple Elementary, and all staff share the responsibility of educating our children in a safe, secure, and orderly environment" (Grinell and Rabin, 2013, p. 760). These focuses being implemented across the elementary further allow Dr. Jordon to shield the teachers under his supervision from the politics behind the education system so that they may solely focus and adhere to the needs of the students.

Maple Elementary exhibits a genuine effort to nurture the students in an environment that allows them to feel empowered by not only their own perseverance but also the school they attend. The school pledges to even allow students to understand their personal responsibility and the role they play in a healthy educational experience. The pledge reads, "As a Maple School student, I know I am the main person in charge of my education. Today is a new day, and I will do my best to act with responsibility. If I want to be respected, I know I need to show respect to others. I am an important person with high goals for myself. I will not let myself or my community down" (Grinell and Rabin, 2013, p. 761). Maple Elementary has truly taken an aggressive step into instituting accountability and respect to peers as a vital process for the students to earn a safe and healthy education. This safeguards a generation of respectful students and peers to have a low rate of bullies and victims in its midst.

Bullying no longer has the stigma that it once had. Nowadays, bullies come in all shapes and sizes and not what they once had a reputation for looking like. Bullies are not only confined to the education system but can be seen in positions of power across our nation, including our former president. The unfortunate truth is that the swiftest way to get away with bullying is through social media and cyberbullying. However, discriminatory bullying has the most variety of bullying due to demographic backgrounds. The effects of bullying are detrimental to American society as some students have endured a lack of humane treatment since beginning in primary education institutions. Should bullying ever meet an end, let it begin in their households, where the mentalities of both bullies and victims are shaped by their parents' sharp or nurturing tongues.

An approach concerned more with a student's well-being rather than a student's ability to perform well on a test might provide guidance to an education system proving its willingness to serve the student as a whole. Maple Elementary leaves a lasting impression of what every parent and student would want their education experiences to be: positive reinforcements and the cultivation of a positive environment. These measures cannot be taken solely by the educator or the student, but a gentle kinship with effort from all those included. Measures taken by Dr. Jordon are as simple as knowing a student's name and reminding them that they matter to the educators (Grinell and Rabin, 2013, p. 759). If more schools take an approach like Maple Elementary, rather than treating the aftermath of bullying, the United States could take a preventative route altogether.

References

Bullying. (2019). In Gale Opposing Viewpoints Online Collection. Gale. https://link.gale.com/apps/doc/PC3010999030/OVIC?u=nm_a_wnmu&sid=OVIC&xid=fa a3dcf

Center for Disease Control and Prevention. (2017). Lesbian, gay, bisexual, and transgender health: Youth. http://www.cdc.gov/lgbthealth/youth.htm.

Gatto, John Taylor. (2008). How Public Education Cripples Our Kids and Why. Yearbook of the National Society for the Study of Education, 107(2), 136–140. https://doi.org/10.1111/j.1744-7984.2008.00183_1.x

Gerstl-Pepin, C. I. (2006). The paradox of Poverty Narratives. Educational Policy, 20(1), 148– 152. https://doi.org/10.1177/0895904805285285

Grinell, S. & Rabin, C. (2013). Modern education: a tragedy of the commons. Journal of Curriculum Studies, 45(6), 760-761. https://doi.org/10.1080/00220272.2013.813079

Hinduja, S. (2018). The ecology of schools: Fostering a culture of human flourishing & developing character. Federal Commission on School Safety. Cyberbully Research Center. https://cyberbullying.org/federal-commission-on-school-safety

Hinduja, S. & Patchin, J. W. (2018). Cyberbullying fact sheet: Identification, prevention, and response. Cyberbullying Research Center. Retrieved 6/11/2019, from https://cyberbullying.org/Cyberbullying-Identification-Prevention-Response- 2018.pdf

John, A., Glendenning, A. C., Marchant, A., Montgomery, P., Stewart, A., Wood, S., . . . Hawton, K. (2018). Self-Harm, Suicidal Behaviours, and Cyberbullying in Children and Young People: Systematic Review. Journal of Medical Internet Research, 20(4), e129. doi:10.2196/jmir.9044

Kosciw, J. G., Greytak, E. A., Zongrone, A. D., Clark, C. M., & Truong, N. L. (2018). The 2017 National School Climate Survey: The experiences of lesbian, gay, bisexual, transgender, and queer youth in our nation's schools. New York: GLSEN. https://www.glsen.org/sites/default/files/GLSEN-2017-National-School-Climate-Survey-NSCS-Full-Report.pdf

National Center for Education Statistics (NCES), U.S. Department of Education. (2016). Student reports of bullying and cyberbullying: Results from the 2015 School Crime Supplement to the National Crime Victimization Survey. https://nces.ed.gov/pubs2017/2017015.pdf

Ray, B. D. (2017). A systematic review of the empirical research on selected aspects of homeschooling as a school choice. Journal of School Choice, 11(4), 604–621. https://doi.org/10.1080/15582159.2017.1395638

Rose, C. A. & Gage, N. A. (2017). Exploring the involvement of bullying among students with disabilities over time. Exceptional Children, 83, 298-314. http://journals.sagepub.com/doi/abs/10.1177/0014402916667587

T. Hartley, Michael & Bauman, Sheri & Nixon, Charisse & Davis, Stan. (2015). Comparative study of bullying victimization among students in general and special education. Exceptional children, 81, 176-193. 10.1177/0014402914551741.

U.S. Department of Education, Office for Civil Rights (OCR). (2019). 2015-16 Civil Rights Data Collection (CRDC). School Climate and Safety. https://www2.ed.gov/about/offices/list/ocr/docs/school-climate-and-safety.pdf

U.S. Department of Health and Human Services/Centers for Disease Control and Prevention (CDC) (2018). Youth Risk Behavior Surveillance—United States, 2017 Morbidity and Mortality Weekly Report (MMWR). (67)8. https://www.cdc.gov/healthyyouth/data/yrbs/pdf/2017/ss6708.pdf

Van Lancker, W. & Parolin, Z. (2020). COVID-19, school closures, and child poverty: a social crisis in the making. The Lancet Public Health, 5(5). https://doi.org/10.1016/s24682667(20)30084-0

Pride and Prejudice **and** *Little Women:*
Loss of Identity Through Marriage
Rachel Layden

ABSTRACT

In Jane Austen's *Pride and Prejudice* and Louisa May Alcott's *Little Women*, there is often a consensus that the stories' heroines get the happy ending they deserve. The following is an analysis on not necessarily what our initial spunky protagonists gain in their romance and marriages, but the trade-off that exists because of the complex dynamic between their loss of identity from who they are initially portrayed as, to what they become as the story progresses. In doing so, each protagonist's setting, partner, and family are taken into account to determine how Lizzy and Jo lose their livelier spirits and morph into characters that reflect the conventions of their time. Lizzy and Jo claim to be content and fulfilled by the end of their respective novels so their change in identities is not personally a loss for them, but as modern readers, we expect a greater fight against conformity that was promised to us through Austen and Alcott's promising portrayals of Lizzy Bennet and Jo March.

"It is a truth universally acknowledged, that a single man in possession of a good fortune, must be in want of a wife" (Austen 5). Jane Austen opens *Pride and Prejudice* with these lines to emphasize how marriage was viewed singularly in nineteenth century England. The protagonists, Elizabeth "Lizzy" Bennet and Fitzwilliam Darcy, struggle to maintain their personal identities while navigating their romance. This proves to be more difficult for Lizzy because of her gender and position in society.

This idea is similarly expressed in Louisa May Alcott's *Little Women*, where the lively Josephine "Jo" March finds it difficult to express her feelings for the serious Professor Bhaer while pursuing her personal writing endeavors. Both heroines are introduced as exceptionally independent and free-spirited women who deviate from the conventions of their given times, only to fall right into conformity when they marry. The initial characterization of Lizzy and Jo sets a standard that cannot be maintained because these women inevitably fall in love with men who influence their identities, and they are limited by the arbitrary social conventions of their time; as readers, we are left with much to the imagination and led to believe that our heroines are fulfilled with their life choices. Lizzy Bennet and Jo March's loss of identities through marriage show that conventions are hard to escape because the institution of marriage is rooted in conformity, thus denying Lizzy and Jo of their individuality because their innate identities contradict the expectations set before them.

The theme of loss of identity through romance/marriage is foreshadowed in the titles of Alcott and Austen's work. The title "*Pride and Prejudice*" refers to the compromises that Darcy and Lizzy commit to: Darcy abandons his prejudice against social inferiority while Elizabeth abandons her pride in defense of Darcy's prejudice against her lower status.

Darcy initially represses his feelings for Lizzy by convincing himself that their differences in social status prevent them from being romantically linked: "...Darcy had never been so bewitched by any woman as he was by her. He really believed, that were it not for the inferiority of her connections, he should be in some danger" (Austen 51). Darcy's seemingly fixed aloofness is shaken.

In contrast, Lizzy's pre-marriage identity is based on free-thinking and confidence that is expressed through witty banter. Lizzy sets aside her ego when she accepts partial responsibility for her and Darcy's disputes and does not attempt to gain the upper hand in their interactions: "We will not quarrel for the greater share of blame . . . but since then, we have both, I hope, improved in civility" (Austen 347). At the time of Lizzy and Darcy's engagement (and afterwards), Lizzy no longer takes pleasure in provoking Darcy because she has happily traded in her playful teasing for genuine affection and admiration for Darcy's ability to compromise.

The title of *Little Women* is an oxymoron that suggests that the March sisters are navigating between adolescence and adulthood. Jo and the March sisters are still impressionable young girls, but they are tasked with important life decisions that affect their future. Jo struggles to find a balance between her love life and her professional ambitions of becoming a writer. Jo's inexperience in both areas makes her more reliant and passive of Professor Bhaer's opinion. Austen describes how Professor Bhaer manipulates Jo's decisions by refusing to nurture her literary aspirations: "…no one observed it but Professor Bhaer. He did it so quietly that Jo never knew he was watching to see if she would accept and profit by his reproof; but she stood the test and he was satisfied, for though no words passed between them, he knew that she had given up writing" (Alcott 348).

Jo's naivete coincides with her pre-marriage identity of spontaneity and stubbornness to relentlessly set out to achieve her goals. Jo admits defeat as an unsuccessful writer but expresses more emotion for leaving Professor Bhaer to return home than for her literary shortcomings.

Alcott and Austen set their characters up for failure by introducing strong-willed women with ambition and moxie who endear readers, only to dramatically change their character arc. Lizzy is introduced as the most outspoken Bennet sister who takes pleasure in teasing her mother for falling victim to the pressures of society and securing her daughters' successful marriages; instead, Lizzy identifies more with her father because they share an indifference to societal expectations. Lizzy's self-confidence is portrayed through her intelligent dialogue as well as her ability to remain dignified when faced with offensive statements. For example, Lizzy receives Darcy's insult that: "She [Lizzy] is tolerable; but not handsome enough to tempt me" as an expression of his own sense of entitlement and snobbery, not a true reflection of her self-worth (Austen 13). Lizzy confides in her friend that she feels indifferent to Darcy's sense of entitlement except when it pertains directly to her, "and I could easily forgive his pride, if he had not mortified mine" (Austen 21). Lizzy prioritizes her pride and self-worth over marriage prospects. Lizzy is aware that Darcy is the most eligible bachelor and there is no denying that she is intrigued by his mystery; however, she is revolted by his sour demeanor. At this point, Lizzy is following her instincts and we applaud how she determines her own self-worth without paying any attention to how she is perceived in the watchful nineteenth century England. Lizzy eventually falls for Darcy, they are wed, and we only see a remnant of her previous identity; it is an abrupt romance.

Elizabeth gains a romantic partnership in marrying Darcy and can eliminate some of her own prejudices by recognizing his experiences and perspectives, but simultaneously, she fails to exercise her own ideas and beliefs, which is her tragic (but often unrecognized) downfall.

Similar in circumstance is Jo March's marriage to Professor Bhaer. Jo is portrayed as the most ambitious and free-spirited March sister who has her sights set on becoming a famous writer. Jo is not just a dreamer; she takes practical steps to carving out a way in the world for herself—and just like Lizzy, this unique sense of identity is overshadowed by the identity that she develops after deciding to prioritize love. Jo and Bhaer's romance is not quite as complex as that of Darcy and Lizzy's. However, it took more explicit convincing for Jo to even consider marriage. Beth inspires

Jo to prioritize love over her desire to write "splendid books" or "seeing all the world": "And then and there Jo renounced her old ambition, pledged herself to a new and better one, acknowledging the poverty of other desires and feeling blessed solace of a belief in the immortality of love" (Alcott 404). From this point forward, Jo represses her natural instincts to honor her sister's dying wishes. Jo's aspirations of writing never return within the story's plot line. Instead, we see Jo focus more on domestic duties which align with her promise to Beth: "Nothing could be more natural or proper than for my Professor to open a school, and for me to prefer to reside on my own estate" (Alcott 464). Jo and Lizzy's tradeoffs for marriage and love are not in and of themselves negative. On the contrary, Lizzy and Jo become more understanding of other characters who are innately conformists. However, these choices deviate from their initial introductions that we have already grown attached to, and we wait in anticipation for how their projected futures will look.

Lizzy and Jo's loss of identity is exemplified in how they begin to morph into their sisters, namely Jane Bennet and Meg March.

Jane and Meg are the eldest sisters in their families who function as the tabula rasa because it is anticipated that they will experience all of life's big moments before their younger siblings; they are most susceptible to being influenced by their environments. Jane and Meg are simple and singular in their purpose in life, which is to marry. Jane's character changes little from the beginning of the story where she courts Bingley, to the middle where she waits for Bingley, and at the end where they are married. Jane and Bingley's marriage is expected and reflects the strong social conformity that Jane has and will always adhere to. Jane's predictability is bland, but she and Bingley are so good-natured and sweet that it is difficult to be too severe on their conformity. We don't expect to see Lizzy follow in Jane's direction in life, but Austen unexpectedly mirrors their post-marriages to be eerily similar by illustrating both women's new role as wives to be greatly influenced by their estates and domestic duties: "Mr. Bingley and Jane remained at Netherfield only a twelve-month. So near a vicinity to her mother and Meryton relations was not desirable even to his easy temper, or her affectionate heart. The darling wish of his sisters was then gratified; he bought an estate in a neighbouring county to Derbyshire, and Jane and Elizabeth, in addition to every other source of happiness, were within thirty miles of each other" (Austen 364). Austen projects this future for Jane from the beginning of the story, but Lizzy's future was supposed to be less predictable. Lizzy walked miles with mud up to her ankles to Longbourn to ensure that Jane was healthy when she became sick visiting Bingley, she rejected the most eligible bachelor on conflicting principles, and was always prepared for friendly banter. The final portrait that we have of Lizzy is not complementary to her pre-marriage identity. Jane already holds the role of the sweet, good-natured domestic sister. We rely on Lizzy to challenge her society's expectations but find that she comes to align more with its conventions over time.

The first indication of Lizzy's loss/change in identity is the absence of intelligent repartee between Darcy and Lizzy. Just as Jane finds no fault in her beau, "He is just what a young man ought to be . . . sensible, good humored, lively; and I never saw such happy manners!- so much ease, with such perfect good breeding!" (Austen 16). Lizzy also seems to forget that Darcy is imperfect and defends his character to Mr. Bennet, "I love him. Indeed he has no improper pride. He is perfectly amiable. You do not know what he really is; then pray do not pain me by speaking of him in such terms" (Austen 356). It is on good authority that Jane is speaking the truth when she describes Bingley as charming as he is because he is universally well-liked. In contrast, Darcy is generally disliked: ". . . his manners gave a disgust which turned the tide of his popularity" (Austen 12). Despite the fact that Darcy later proves to have redeeming qualities (securing a deal with Wickham to salvage Lydia's reputation) that make Lizzy's affection for him understandable, it is still unsettling for Lizzy to describe him in such an inaccurate way. Lizzy's loss of identity begins with confusion in her judgment by exchanging any necessary prejudice that helped her develop conclusions about people for a pacifistic perception of the world.

Jo also begins to morph into her older sister. Meg is adored for her gentle demeanor and desire to find love and start a family of her own, which is hysterical because at one point, Jo is so opposed to Meg being married to John so young that she proposes the following to Marmee, "I knew there was mischief brewing, I felt it, and now it's worse than I imagined. I just wish I could marry Meg myself, and keep her safe in the family" (Alcott 199). Jo is so protective and territorial of her family that you might mistake her leadership as a requisite for the role held as the eldest sister in the March clan who looks over the younger girls. However, the docile Meg is the eldest, and she, along with Beth's sweet nature, manages to have a profound influence on Jo's decision to marry Professor Bhaer and eventually lose part of her identity.

These ideas of love and marriage are implanted in Jo's mind as one of Beth's last dying wishes, "You must take my place, Jo, and be everything to Father and Mother when I'm gone. They will turn to you, don't fail them . . . for love is the only thing that we can carry with us when we go, and it makes the end so easy" (Alcott 404).

Jo accepts these conditions, though these beliefs interfere with Jo's previous goals of achieving autonomy and success to selflessly provide for her family: "Though very happy in the social atmosphere about her, and very busy with the daily work that earned her bread and made it sweeter for the effort, Jo still found time for literary labors. The purpose which now took possession of her was a natural one to a poor and ambitious girl, but the means she took to gain her end were not the best. She saw that money conferred power: money and power, therefore she resolved to have, not to be used for herself alone, but for those she loved more than self" (Alcott 336). The ambitions that came naturally to Jo were already serving the needs of her family and were done with love, so Beth's advice to Jo is ultimately serving the same purpose, but it demands that Jo sacrifice her ambitions for what is implied to be marriage. Jo begins to deviate from her goals of becoming a writer and begins to consider beginning a life like Meg's: "Marriage is an excellent thing, after all. I wonder if I should blossom out half as well as you have, if I tried it?" (Alcott 419). Meg reinforces these ideas in Jo: "she felt it her duty to enforce her opinion by every argument in her power, and the sisterly chats were not wasted, especially as two of Meg's most effective arguments were the babies, whom Jo loved tenderly" (Alcott 419). As Jo allows Meg to talk into her ear, she gradually begins to lose her position as the initiator in the family, instead choosing to take advice rather than learning from her own endeavors. And much like undeniable parallels between Lizzy and Jane at the end of *Pride and Prejudice*, Jo's life and identity come to resemble Meg's because of how dramatically her identity changes from an ambitious free spirit to one that is content with convention. Jo abandons her own goals and designs her life around Professor Bhaer's career by acting like an assistant to his career as an educator. Jo still maintains more autonomy compared to Meg because she inherits Plumfield and makes the final decision to convert the estate into a school (rather than choose to live in it, as Meg would be expected to do), but it is frustrating to imagine how Jo would have used Plumfield had it not been for Meg and Beth's influence on Jo's shift in identity from a nomadic spirit to a grounded wife.

Darcy and Professor Bhaer also serve as direct influences on Lizzy and Jo's loss of identities. Darcy and Bhaer serve as Lizzy and Jo's opposites who tame their more unconventional behaviors and beliefs. Darcy has shamelessly presented himself as such a pompous prude that Lizzy has to reassure her family that she does in fact have feelings for Darcy when they announce their engagement: "At night she opened her heart to Jane. Though suspicion was very far from Miss Bennet's general habits, she was absolutely incredulous here" (Austen 352). Lizzy's out-of-character behavior is so obscure that it motivates all the Bennets to intervene in ways that are out of character for them as well: Jane confronts Lizzy about her judgment and reveals Bingley's lack of confidence in the possibility of the match between Lizzy and Darcy by saying: "Nothing could give either Bingley or myself [Jane] more delight. But we considered it, we talked of it as impossible. And do you really love him quite well enough? Oh, Lizzy! Do any thing rather than marry without affection. Are you quite sure that you feel what you ought to do?" (Austen 353). Even Mr. Bennet feels it necessary to confront his favorite child to ensure that Lizzy is willingly and happily accepting Darcy's proposal: "Are you out of your senses to be accepting this man? Have not you always hated him?" (Austen 355). The Bennets' response to Lizzy's engagement is reasonable. The only side of Darcy that they (and the rest of Longbourn) have witnessed, has been consistently unpleasant. Upon Darcy's introduction at the Meryton ball, there is a general consensus that he is unpleasant: ". . . he was discovered to be proud, to be above his company, and above being pleased; and not all his large estate in Derbyshire could then save him from having a most forbidding, disagreeable countenance, and being unworthy to be compared with his friend" (Austen 17). The Bennets fear that Lizzy will be unhappy with Darcy as a husband. It takes repeated questioning and reassurance from Lizzy for the Bennets to be put at ease that Lizzy happily consents to the marriage. The reservations that the Bennets have of Darcy do not paint him in a flattering light and elicit discussion over his and Lizzy's compatibility. It is asking a lot of an audience to accept that Lizzy is suddenly professing her feelings for a man with whom she has had so many fundamental disagreements with. It would be more convincing if Lizzy explained that she loved Darcy in spite of their differences, but she insists that he is "perfectly amiable" and has "no improper pride." Darcy never surrenders his pride when Lizzy rejects his first proposal. Darcy's strategy in confessing his love to Lizzy is to explain the reasons why marrying her would be beneath him, but in his thought process, this is a romantic and appropriate approach. Darcy does not even have the humility to accept Lizzy's rejection with grace: "And this is all the reply which I am to have the honour of expecting! I might, perhaps, wish to be informed why, with so little endeavour at civility, I am thus rejected. But it is of small importance" (Austen 186). Darcy tries to reproach Lizzy, but it is to his own demise because Lizzy is not so forgiving of his insolence, "I might as well enquire why with so evident a design of offending and insulting me, you chose to tell me that you liked me against your will, against your reason, and even against your character? Was not this some excuse for incivility, if I was uncivil? But I have other provocations. You know I have. Had not my own feelings decided against you, had they been indifferent, or had they even been favourable, do you think that any consideration would tempt me to accept the man, who has been the means of ruining, perhaps for ever, the happiness of a most beloved sister?" (Austen 186). This is the assertive and confrontational Lizzy who is unblinded by Darcy's flaws and who can eloquently express how his false sense of superiority is unbecoming. Darcy respects these qualities in Lizzy, but he is unwilling to admit this or stop himself from hurting her: "I have no wish of denying that I did everything in my power to separate my friend from your sister, or that I rejoice in my success. Towards him I have been kinder than towards myself" (Austen 187). Darcy's ill attempt to fall on his sword does not satisfy Lizzy because she is not superficial or simple. Lizzy understands the importance of protecting loved ones but does not excuse his shamelessness in wounding Jane and herself in the process. Darcy's lack of tact is repulsive. Lizzy's rejection of his first proposal reflects her strong sense of identity and self-worth, but when she accepts his second proposal, there is still no resolution or remorse expressed for Darcy's interference in Jane and Bingley's relationship. To someone so bright and assertive as Lizzy, it is expected that these kinds of loose ends be rectified, but alas, Lizzy does not hold Darcy accountable for these faults when she accepts his second proposal, and Darcy takes advantage of this by gaslighting Lizzy into thinking that she has miscalculated his character: "For, though your accusations were ill-founded, formed on mistaken premises, my behavior to you at the time, had merited the severest reproof" (Austen 347). Darcy disguises this gaslighting tactic as self-deprecation. At this point, Lizzy is already too smitten to notice these subtle manipulations, but Darcy is aware of how the early establishment of this control over Lizzy's mind will work to his advantage into their marriage. Darcy has redeeming qualities, but Lizzy has always had to initiate that he admits to his faults. He is not a self-starter in this way, so when she finally accepts his second proposal (and does not demand any explanation for any past faults) he does not offer any reflection or remorse.

Darcy displays love and affection for Lizzy, but he still prioritizes himself over anyone else. He carries a level of narcissism that demands that the people around him, especially those willing to be around him, cater to him rather than themselves. Professor Bhaer represents the same deficiencies as Darcy in that he values his opinion and intellect over his affection for Jo. Jo is immediately taken with Bhaer and respects his intelligence, humility, and strong values of decency; in this respect, it is unfair to liken Darcy and Bhaer's characters. However, Bhaer's magnificence in Jo's eyes does make her susceptible to pleasing him by adjusting her goals to align more with his beliefs. For example, Bhaer not only shows a disapproval of Jo writing sensational stories, but also uses the anecdote, "There is a demand for whisky, but I think you and I do not care to sell it. If the respectable people knew what harm they did, they would not feel that the living was honest. They haf no right to put poison in the sugarplum, and let the small ones eat it. No, they should think a little, and sweep mud in the street before they do this thing" (Alcott 346). Bhaer's ethical approach to life is noble and unwavering, while Jo's is spontaneous and evolving. Bhaer's influence on Jo unknowingly hinders her writing goals because instead of taking her usual approach of writing what she can sell, she tries to fit into a niche where she does not belong, "Jo wrote no more sensational stories, deciding that the money did not pay for her share of the sensation, but going to the other extreme, as is the way with people of her stamp, she took a course of Mrs. Sheerwood, Miss Edgeworth, and Hannah More, and then produced a tale which might have been more properly called an essay or a sermon, so intensely moral was it" (Alcott 347). Bhaer encourages Jo to not sacrifice her morals for money, but what he does not account for is how Jo's lack of publications directly affects her writing entirely because she has not abandoned her goals to fiscally support her family.

Writing has always been Jo's dream, a career that she aspired to achieve, but her admiration and affection for Bhaer unconsciously changes Jo's plans, and she accepts that if she cannot achieve it in a way that Bhaer approves of, she will not write at all, "Well, the winter's gone, and I've written no books, earned no fortune, but I've made a friend worth having and I'll try to keep him all my life" (Alcott 349). Jo has already determined that her relationship with Bhaer is more valuable than her personal aspirations, which is a great shift in Jo's life and identity because writing and ambition have long been her passions, not just a fleeting interest. Bhaer is too consumed in his own purpose of education and charity to recognize how his stern influence affects Jo's life. Darcy and Bhaer positively challenge Lizzy and Jo by acting as their opposites, but this does not necessarily make them compatible companions, especially when you consider how the union of marriage will compound the complication of their dynamics.

Lizzy and Jo's identities suffer from the limitations of their environments. Lizzy and Jo do not have many opportunities to gain perspective before marrying because they are limited by temporal and social formalities. Jo fortunately has the advantage of having a supportive male friend in Laurie to model what it means to encourage her individuality. Laurie loves Jo so much that he is willing to sacrifice his own identity to make Jo happy, "If you loved me, Jo, I should be a perfect saint, for you could make me anything you like" (Alcott 353). Laurie and Jo's lengthy friendship accounts for understanding her so well that he even predicts that Jo is enamored by Professor Bhaer and with that knowledge, he is still willing to be with Jo and do what he can to encourage her aspirations: "I only loved you all the more, and I worked hard to please you, and I gave up billiards and everything you didn't like, and waited and never complained, for I hoped you'd love me, though I'm not half good enough . . ." (Alcott 352).

Although Jo cannot genuinely reciprocate these feelings for Laurie, these experiences serve as a representation of Jo's evolving perception of what marriage ought to be: ". . . you and I are not suited to each other, because our quick tempers and strong wills would probably make us very miserable . . . and I won't risk our happiness by such a serious experiment . . ." (Alcott 353). We are accustomed to Jo's spontaneity and affection for Laurie, so it is disappointing to not see them happily united in marriage. However, Jo's decision to not marry Laurie reflects her growing maturity that she has learned from the mellow Bhaer.

Unfortunately, Lizzy does not have anyone to model such unconditional (romantic) love for her before she marries Darcy, so she unknowingly settles for him. To her disadvantage, Lizzy has only had worse prospects, Wickham and Mr. Collins. Wickam is a deceitful fraud and Mr. Collins is embarrassingly foolish. These prospects do nothing to raise her standards for marriage and she refuses to act by design and marry out of security. Of course, by the time she is engaged to Darcy and married, she is naive to what a healthy marriage entails because her parents' relationship is inequitable. Other marriages in *Pride and Prejudice* are direct consequences of marrying out of necessity. Charlotte Lucas best exemplifies marrying out of necessity by explaining to Lizzy that securing marriage is strategic: ". . . it is sometimes a disadvantage to be so very guarded. If a woman conceals her affection with the same skill from the object of it, she may lose the opportunity of fixing him; and it will then be but poor consolation to believe the world equally in the dark" (Austen 22). Charlotte offers Lizzy a pragmatic view of marriage that will come to serve as an explanation for her own marriage to Mr. Collins. Lizzy does not exercise Charlotte's advice, but she does consider how it applies generally to life and marriage. Lizzy becomes more exposed to different perspectives and uses new information to gradually shift her identity from one of innate principles to welcoming variance.

To Charlotte Lucas's point, the time and setting of both *Pride and Prejudice* and *Little Women* portray the enormous amount of social pressure that women experience as they live in societies where marriage is expected and necessary in securing their well-being. This is especially important for Lizzy and the other female characters in Pride and Prejudice because their gender prevents them from inheriting familial property, "Mr. Bennet's property consisted almost entirely in an estate of two thousand a year, which, unfortunately for his daughters was entailed in default of heirs male, on a distant relation; and their mother's fortune, though ample for her situation in life, could but ill supply the deficiency of his" (Austen 29). These institutional injustices show that Lizzy is aware of both implicit and explicit consequences of her marriage to Darcy. Even with Charlotte's advice in mind, Lizzy is not someone who subjects herself to uncomfortable situations. For example, Lizzy is aware of how Caroline Bingley does not accept her into their exclusive social group, and she jumps at every opportunity to distance herself from them, even on casual strolls, "No, no; stay where you are. You are charmingly group'd and appear to uncommon advantage. The picturesque would be spoilt by admitting a fourth. Good bye" (Austen 52). Rather than remain in unwelcomed territory at Netherfield, Lizzy feels the urgency to return home as soon as Jane feels well because she is worldly and recognizes that her behavior and identity greatly deviates from the conformity that is expected upon entering an estate like Meryton. So, if Lizzy can barely withstand temporary visits to Meryton, it is hard to imagine that she would subject herself to living a married life at Pemberley where people like Lady Catherine relentlessly try to overestimate their importance by imposing on people's liberties: "Miss Bennet, I am shocked and astonished. I expected to find a more reasonable young woman. But do not deceive yourself into a belief that I will ever recede. I shall not go away, till you have given me the assurance I require" (Austen 337).

Lizzy brilliantly gets the better of Lady Catherine by arguing that any potential marriage to Darcy is out of Lady Catherine's control and solely based on her own consent and Darcy's willingness to neglect any of Lizzy's lack of 'connections': "Whatever my connections may be, if your nephew does not object to them, they can be nothing to you " (Austen 337). Lizzy defends herself well, but unfortunately, Lady Catherine's threat is fated to be a thorn in Lizzy's side and is just the first of many implicit disapprovals that are awaiting Lizzy after she marries Darcy. Lizzy might be able to endure this, except that her real life would not be an endless battle of wits. Instead, what we can assume is that Lizzy lives the rest of her life having to endure high society events where she is criticized for things that are out of her control, namely her "humble" beginnings. This would inevitably impact Lizzy's psyche over time because class and status are so prevalent in Lizzy's time.

Jo's submission to social conformity is more in part to her appreciation for convention rather than the pressure of it. Jo does not encounter an equivalent of Lady Catherine in Concord, nor does she share as pragmatic of an outlook on marriage as Charlotte Lucas, but she does begin to appreciate what marriage offers instead of what it compromises: ". . . the life I wanted then seems selfish, lonely, and cold to me now. I haven't given up the hope that I may write a good book yet, but I can wait, and I'm sure it will all be the better for such experiences and illustrations as these . . . There's no need for me to say it, for everyone can see that I'm far happier than I deserve" (Alcott 471). Jo happily dotes on her "good husband" and her "chubby children" and holds on to her aspirations to write but does not feel a void having not fulfilled her personal endeavors yet (Alcott 471).

Alcott and Austen are responsible for Lizzy and Jo's shortcomings and loss of identities because their control over the narratives of *Pride and Prejudice* and *Little Women* is contradicted by their own strong adherence to their identities.

Alcott and Austen famously never married during their lifetimes but did pursue their ambitions. Alcott and Austen both wrote several novels, so it seems unfair and strange that they did not fully commit to modeling their personal experiences into the portrayal of Lizzy or Jo. More specifically, modern readers are often disappointed that Jo March marries at all in *Little Women*. Alcott originally planned for Jo to remain unwed, but she was pressured by publishers to give Jo a more conventional ending; this was believed to be a better selling point for the novel and Alcott conceded.

Alcott remains responsible for Jo's lackluster arc because she consciously wrote her story to satisfy the general audience, not to provoke them or defy conventions herself. Sands-O'Connor explains that Alcott was so insulted by the criticism she received for her views (in previous publications) that marital separation should be condoned when love no longer exists that she raged in her journal: "My next book shall have no ideas in it, only facts and the people shall be as ordinary as possible, then critics will say it is all right" (Sands-O'Connor). Jo's "happily ever after" at the expense of losing part of her free-spirited identity is only satisfactory to nineteenth century readers who were conditioned to believe that Jo had to sacrifice her ambitious endeavors to commit to a happy relationship with Professor Bhaer. Today's readers are more inclined to find fault with Jo's abandonment of her literary aspirations because it is generally believed that it is possible to strike a work/life balance and that one's identity should be preserved/enhanced, not replaced.

Lizzy Bennet allows Darcy to influence her into submission; Lizzy was initially outspoken and formed her own opinions, but towards the end of the novel, Lizzy is more agreeable to Darcy's principles and lifestyle. Their life at Pemberley marks a new era for Lizzy's transition into conformity.

Jo March also experiences a trade-off with her identity from independent dreamer to grounded wife/mother whose role is to support her husband and raise her children. Lizzy and Jo come to reflect the values of their times instead of challenging their society's expectations. These changes in identity are exacerbated by the influence that Darcy and Bhaer have on the leading heroines because they serve as opposites to the versions of that who Lizzy and Jo eventually become. It is not fundamentally wrong for Lizzy and Jo to follow more conventional paths in life, but it is disappointing to witness their diminishing identities that they originally enticed the audience with.

Bibliography

Alcott, Louisa May, and Camille Cauti. Little Women. Barnes & Noble Classics, 2005.
Austen, Jane, and Vivien Jones. Pride and Prejudice. Penguin Books, 2005.
Sands-O'Connor, Karen. "Why Jo Didn't Marry Laurie: Louisa May Alcott and The Heir of Redclyffe(1)." ATQ: 19th century American literature and culture, vol. 15, no. 1, Mar. 2001.

Oedipus Wreck

Tomas Marrufo

ABSTRACT

This paper examines the role of six fathers over three works of literature. By examining these fathers and their myriad of failures, we can see the damage that is wrought by failed implementations of fatherhood. The first section covers fathers and the mistakes that they make as they implement their own ideas of paternity. The second section covers the emotional damage that unsuccessful fatherhood creates. The last section examines the role of archetypal fathers in a classic play to examine dynamics between fathers and their children. Throughout the paper, attention is also brought to the role of maternal forces in the relationships that are covered.

Fatherhood has historically been the odd man out when it comes to serious discussion of parenthood. The role of mothers in society, and perhaps rightly so, is often covered much more thoroughly. After several dozen hours in literature classes, I have come to realize that the shift of focus away from fathers and onto mothers is incredibly odd. Throughout my college career, there have been numerous books that were driven by the failure of a father figure. These men often served as the impetus for the protagonist's journeys, growth, or failures. The impact of these father figures shows that fatherhood is profoundly important in the development of children. Good fathers can uplift and help their children live successful lives. Those that fail their children forsake them to a life of hardship and turmoil. The ruination of children by archetypal failing fathers is often so complete that the child is faced with diminished quality of life, and sometimes, damage so detrimental that the life of the child is forever altered.

Fatherhood has served as a primary motivator in literature for as long as it has existed. The Common Era is full of stories of heroes and villains who were incited into action by the successes and failures of their fathers. These failed men have created just as many archetypes and tropes as they have actual children. The villain, the victim, the hero, and the savior are all archetypal characters that are often driven by a failed father. Frankenstein's monster, who was amalgamated in 1817, was driven primarily from the failure of his father. The abandonment and hatred of Frankenstein's creature completely stunted his development. This failure created one of the clearest examples of the archetypal victim in all of literature. Some sixteen hundred years before Shakespeare created the hero of heroes, the Christian savior Jesus Christ was put to a brutal death. His last words were a lamentation of the abandonment of his own father, the ultimate patriarchal archetype.

The distance in time between the works covered in this essay shows that the issue of failed fathers has been a common concern for well over a millennium. The differences in culture and even gender between the three authors also show that fatherhood is a long reaching subject. These works are very different, but their characteristics weave them together into a tapestry that contains similar messages. The main characteristic that remains similar in each of these examples of fatherhood is the lack of maternal figures. Mothers exist in a ghostly fashion throughout these works, but their roles are negligible next to actions incited by fathers. The successes and failures that are examined will give us pause as we examine questions that have existed for much longer than these works. Is the successful implementation of fatherhood possible without the presence of a maternal figure, and is fatherhood without maternal guidance possible, or would that be a subversion of fatherhood?

Silas Marner, which was written by George Eliot in 1861, is a fine place to begin examining fatherhood. The work features two fathers who exist on separate sides of the good father/bad father dichotomy. By examining these fathers and comparing their similarities and differences, we will reach a deeper understanding of the impact of both men's implementation of fatherhood. The appearance of two fathers in this work is paralleled in the other works covered in this essay. The common thread of multiple fathers will allow us a much wider scope through which we may view fatherhood and its various successes and failures. The two fathers that appear in *Silas Marner* both fulfill the same function as father characters, but their experience and their implementation of fatherhood is completely different from one another.

Godfrey Cass is the first father to be covered, and he serves as an example of the bad father archetype. More specifically, he serves as an example of the unwilling father figure.

In comparison with the other father in this work, Godfrey serves as an example of a more traditional archetypal father. He is misguided in his implementation of fatherhood, and it irrevocably changes his daughter's life. Godfrey, in his youthful abandon, mistakenly marries an opium addict named Molly Farren. Despite being the well-off son from a high-class family, Godfrey is unwilling to admit to his marriage or accept his daughter. This unacceptance stands in stark contrast to that of Molly, who manages to continue her parental duties to some extent despite her horrific circumstances. "Molly knew that the cause of her dirty rags was not husband's neglect, but the demon Opium to whom she was enslaved, body and soul, except in the lingering mother's tenderness that refused to give him her hungry child" (Eliot 107). Molly has nothing, yet she is still willing to love and care for her child. This display of love may be unconventional, but it shows that her natural maternal instincts are much stronger than the natural paternal instincts of Godfrey. While Godfrey fails as a father here, there is an irony in his failure. The negligence of Godfrey directly leads his daughter, Eppie, towards a better life. In disowning Eppie, Godfrey unknowingly gives her a caring and nourishing father that is the polar opposite of Godfrey himself. Godfrey's first act of good parenting is done unintentionally, but still causes miraculous consequences for Eppie.

Godfreys's lack of any parental responsibility can be traced to a definitive source, which is the circumstances of his own broken family. His mother died when he was young, and that indirectly changed the dynamics of his family.

For the Squire's wife had died long ago, and the Red House was without that presence of the wife and mother which is the fountain of wholesome love and fear in parlor and kitchen; and this helped to account not only for the frequency with which the proud Squire condescended to preside in the parlor of the Rainbow rather than under the shadow of his own wainscot; perhaps, also, for the fact that his sons had turned out rather ill (Eliot 33). The death of Squire Cass's wife is the beginning of the Squire's failure as a father. Rather than spending time with his children, he begins to spend his time at the local tavern. Squire's responsibility as a father died with his wife. The mother's death was damaging enough, but their father's complete negligence serves as a continuing source of trauma for the young boys. The damage of this negligence is visible in both Godfrey and Dunstan. Both men are broken and incapable of caring for anyone other than themselves. Godfrey shows the extent of this damage when later in the novel he discusses his understanding of his father's uncaring nature. "The old Squire was an implacable man: he made resolution in violent anger, and he was not to be moved from them after his anger had subsided . . . He was not critical of the faulty indulgence which preceded these fits; that seemed to him natural enough" (Eliot 60). Godfrey was not raised correctly due to the lack of a mother and his father's abandonment. He looks at his father's character flaws with acceptance because he has never witnessed good parenting, which would have shown him what he should have had. These obvious character flaws have become an unfortunate norm for Godfrey that he eventually begins to mimic in his own role as a father.

However, Godfrey does change course from his original archetypal role to that of an archetype reaching for the good father role. His reasoning for this change is seriously misguided, but it does make sense for someone who was raised outside of a family consisting of two loving parents. "And that other child, not on the hearth-he would not forget it; he would see that it was well provided for. That was a father's duty" (Eliot, 152). Godfrey has no understanding of the maternal contributions to a family, so he resorts to the purely paternal instincts that he witnessed in his father growing up. He reduces the role of fatherhood to a role that exists only to financially provide for children.

The emotional understanding that his mother would have provided for him, and that Silas provides for Eppie, is completely missing from Godfrey's point of view.

Silas, on the other hand, exists as an example of a good father. He does not exist as an archetypal father; he does not even exist as an archetypal man. "In the day when the spinning-wheels hummed busily in the farmhouses . . . there might be seen in districts far away among the lanes, or deep in the bosom of the hills, certain pallid undersized men, who, by the side of the brawny country-folk, looked like the remnants of a disinherited race" (Eliot 1). Silas's lack of paternal or male characteristics would be considered a character flaw in many different scenarios, especially during this time when men fit into a very narrow definition of masculinity. For a time before he meets his future daughter, he does suffer because of his weaver's role as an un-masculine member of a disinherited race. Children look at Silas with equal parts wonder and pity. The people of Raveloe view him as a sad example of a man who has never achieved anything of note.

Silas's first life in the hyper-religious community of Lantern Yard is punctuated by a complete betrayal by his more conventionally masculine friend. Through jealousy and trickery, Silas is driven from the community that has served as the only home he ever knew. His total faith in God is shattered when he is banished from the community. "There is no just God that governs the earth righteously, but a God of lies, that bears witness against the innocent" (Eliot 22). Silas serves as a harsh example of what the failure of a father can inflict on a child, even if that failure is entirely self-perceived. Silas feels that he is abandoned by God, and this feeling ruins him utterly. He goes from being a man of the community with strong conviction, to being a man who lives only for the basest of desires. "But at night came his revelry: at night he closed his shutters, and made fast his doors, and drew forth his gold . . . He loved the guineas best . . . the guineas that were only half earned by the work in his loom, as if they had been unborn children" (Eliot 21). Silas's obsession with his hoard serves as one of the only examples of Silas exhibiting more "traditionally" male characteristics. He feels the need to maintain and covet his gold in a manner that is as damaging as the unthinking spending of Squire Cass.

This masculine quality is hidden from all and serves as Silas's main character flaw. It is evident that this flaw is known to Silas as he goes through great lengths to hide his obsession from the community. To the community, Silas exists as a strange character, and one that is not fully masculine. Outwardly, his downfall changes his character. The Silas that exists in Raveloe is more of a crone. This outward change to a more feminine role could serve as foreshadowing that his role as a parent will be markedly more maternal than paternal.

Eppie enters Silas's life in an event that saves him from certain doom. The loss of his hoard threatens to ruin him completely. Eppie's sudden and God-given appearance brings about an ultimate change in Silas. "As the child's mind was growing into knowledge, his mind was growing into memory, as her life unfolded, his soul, long stupefied in an old narrow prison, was unfolding, too, and trembling gradually into full consciousness" (Eliot 145). Eppie's appearance incites Silas's recovery from the damage of his youth. Silas's early attempts at parenting are confused and afraid. His time as a solitary figure has blunted his ability to connect with others. He does not have a firm grasp of his own needs, so the needs of a child are as alien to him as a mother's affection is to Godfrey. He is initially able to only provide his child with the shelter and physical stability that the Cass family views as the telltale signs of peak fatherhood. Silas might have faltered in his parental responsibilities without the maternal presence of Dolly Winthrop. Dolly appears towards the beginning of Silas's and Eppie's relationship and becomes a pivotal member of their family. Initially, Silas is wary of Dolly and her influence on this child. "I'll be glad if you'll tell me things. But . . . I want to do things for it myself, else it may get fond o' somebody else, and not fond o'me" (Eliot 123).

This feeling of paternal jealousy exists as a lingering effect of the betrayals that Silas has endured. The thought of losing this child that looks only to him for its needs is too much for him to handle. Dolly's steadfast nature presents Silas with examples of parenting that he uses with great success. His willingness to allow Dolly, and eventually the larger community, access to his daughter's upbringing shows that he cares more about his daughter's life than he does his place as her father. This nurturing appearance of fatherhood exists in stark contrast to the negligence displayed by either of the Cass men.

Silas Marner succeeds as a father not because of his paternal instincts, but because he lacks them. He provides for his daughter in the traditional manner associated by fathers, but he also provides for her emotionally. Silas synergizes both paternal and maternal aspects into his parenting which results in a successful implementation of fatherhood. Silas is especially intriguing. Out of all the fathers in this essay, he stands as the finest example of "good fatherhood." However, this is not an example of successful fatherhood existing without the presence of a maternal figure. Silas's maternal instincts are not exactly God-given; it is also important to view the character of Dolly as a sort of surrogate for both Silas and Eppie. It is not a stretch to say that his "daughter" is raised by not one, but two characters who fall into maternal categories.

From nineteenth century England, we continue walking the trail of failed fathers. This path takes us to the heart of the American Midwest in the mid-1900s. *The Folded Leaf*, written 86 years following *Silas Marner*, also examines the role of fathers in the lives of their children. Despite being written so long after *Silas Marner*, many of the themes and even the failings of the fathers remain similar to the two complicated fathers of Raveloe. *Silas Marner* provides us with a look into what drives two men's implementation of fatherhood. *The Folded Leaf* shows us the damage that two boys incur due in large part to the failures of their fathers. Through the examination of their shared trauma, we can view the damage of fatherhood much more completely.

The two fathers in *The Folded Leaf* do not exist in the same easily defined dichotomy as the fathers from the previous work. Neither Mr. Peters nor Mr. Latham can be described as a good father. They both have flaws that damage their children. Mr. Latham does not have the caring nature of Silas, nor the concrete success of Godfrey. "Evans Latham was an honest and capable man. He had worked hard all his life, and with no other thought to provide for his family, but somehow things never turned out for him the way that they should have" (Maxwell 25). Mr. Latham is naturally ineffectual; despite his arduous work, he never truly finds the success that he looks for. Mr. Latham most closely resembles Silas in the way he has lived his life. Silas was also ineffectual for a long period of his life. However, Silas chose not to succeed due to his fear of society and his lack of trust in people. Mr. Latham fails despite not having the deeply ingrained trauma that pushes Silas to forsake success and society. "It was not the work of his enemies (he had none) and must therefore have been caused by a disembodied malignancy" (Maxwell 25). It is for this reason that his failure can be viewed as much more of a character defect. Despite being set close to a hundred years after *Silas Marner*, the conventional role of fathers remains relatively similar. Fathers were still primarily viewed as paternal caregivers during this period, and they were still looked at for protection and financial support. Spud must see this defect in his father. The adolescent understanding of his father's shortcoming serves as the impetus for Spud's need to control other men through physical violence. By dominating other men, Spud feels he can avoid inheriting his father's ineffectual nature. This need to destroy himself so that he does not turn out like his father is the first evidence of the damage Mr. Latham inflicts upon his son. Spud shows that his immaturity is never curbed by his father's guidance.

Spud's relationship with his father, like that of Godfrey and Squire Cass, is defined by a lack of communication. Mr. Latham is completely unaware of his son's emotions. His failure as a provider results in a move to Chicago, which Spud views as a negative. Mr. Latham sees that his son is struggling in this unfamiliar environment, but he is unable to grasp why Spud has become so angry and closed off. "First time I ever knew you to make a remark like that . . . Are your bowels clogged up" (Maxwell 27). Mr. Latham is unable to effectively connect with any member of his family. He eventually starts to connect with his son over the hyper-masculine sport of boxing, but the physical price that this connection costs takes an eventual toll on Spud. The connection over boxing only serves to bolster the worst qualities in Spud, as it acts as validation for his youthful domination over other boys. Like the Old Squire, Mr. Latham has concluded that his place as a father and as a husband begins and ends at the physical and monetary stability that he is able to provide. Any problems that exist outside of his narrow view of fatherhood are either not understood or pushed aside as a non-issue. Seeing his family dealing poorly with this sudden move, he is not impelled by feelings of comfort and love, but instead by perturbation and indignation. ". . . it's very annoying to come home at the end of a hard day and find all of you glum and dissatisfied . . . it is the best I can provide for you . . . And until you learn to accept it gracefully, maybe you better not come to the table" (Maxwell 27).

Spud's relationship with his father is fraught from the onset of the novel. The presence of his mother serves as a bulwark against the worst of the emotional trauma that the relationship could inflict on Spud if it were left unchecked.

The emotional understanding that is not found in Mr. Latham is readily available in Spud's mother. She wonders to herself what the move will do to her son's mental health. "His face, freed for the time being of both suspicion and misery, was turned towards the ceiling . . . it was a great pity that they had to leave Wisconsin where they knew everybody and the children had so many friends" (Maxwell 21). Both fathers in *The Folded Leaf* have paternal habits that are damaging. The addition of a maternal figure in the form of Spud's mother presents us with a parental unit that, while not perfect, is still much more capable of raising children than Lymie's single father ever could be.

Lymie is damaged terribly by the lack of a maternal figure in his life. Both boys are traumatized by their fathers, but Lymie is almost ruined by the single father that raises him. Mr. Peters is a terrible father. He is, by far, the most damaging father in this novel. Mr. Peters is driven primarily by his libido as well as his immaturity. "The young man had never for one second deserted Mr. Peters. He was always there, tugging at Mr. Peters' elbow, making him do things that were not becoming in a man of forty-five" (Maxwell 32). The women he brings into his life motivate him more than his responsibility as a father. Lymie's father is also a drunk: "his bloodshot eyes and the slight trembling of his hands were evidence that Mr. Peters drank more than was good for him" (Maxwell 32). This man's two vices collide viciously and leave Lymie with a father that is slowly deteriorating in a state of arrested development. Despite being quite young, Mr. Peters appears much older than he actually is. The drinking and hedonism that he partakes in cost him and his son a great deal. "Time is probably no more unkind to sporting characters than it is to other people, but physical decay unsustained by respectability is somehow more noticeable" (Maxwell 32).

Like Mr. Latham, Lymie's father presents us with a man who does not meet the expectations of fatherhood that are viewed as normal in twentieth century America. For all their differences, this is the area in which both men are most similar. Mr. Peters is incapable of emotionally connecting with his son, similar to Mr. Latham's relationship with Spud. Lymie is very young, but he understands implicitly that his father is not motivated by him. "He decided that it wasn't anything that would interest his father . . . if he tried now, his father would make an attempt at listening but his eyes would grow vague, or he would glance away for a second and hardly notice when Lymie stopped talking" (Maxwell 33). This abandonment by his father is much more damaging than Lymie even knows. It is obvious that Lymie's emotional development has been stunted as he grows older. Childish things like candy apples and toy pigs in a window become destabilizing distractions that Lymie is unable to escape from: "He looked in at them until the big round clock on the wall of the butcher shop released him from this trap for children and sent him running down the street" (Maxwell 51). He constantly partakes in childish actions in the vain hope that someone will recognize and validate him in a way that his father never has.

The damage caused by Mr. Peter's lackluster attempt at fatherhood is far-reaching. Lymie has problems connecting with people for the majority of his life. His connection with Spud is so important to him because he has managed to make a connection despite his trauma. Lymie also has problems with the opposite sex. The root of this problem stems back to Lymie's witnessing his father womanize and reduce women down to sexualized objects. "Lymie, who had observed his father bending forward slightly so that he could see inside the neckline of Irma's uniform, said nothing." (Maxwell 39). In the same way that the flawed paternal performance by the Old Squire determined the way Godfrey would eventually view fatherhood, witnessing his father devalue women has left Lymie with the impression that this is the correct way to view the opposite sex. "Here in this long dimly lighted room, where everyone had a price mark attached to him, he recognized Sally's value for the first time" (Maxwell 150). Lymie's attachment of an arbitrary self-created value onto people, especially women, shows that he has developed issues with his views of the opposite sex. Lymie is insecure in his interactions with women, but he is not a user of women like his father. The damaging relationships he saw his father in with random women further feed into Lymie's arrested development. He becomes timid and ineffectual towards women as the story progresses. His father helped to create this inaction towards women, and it is the same inaction that eventually threatens his relationship with Spud.

Lymie and Spud both have disappointing and ineffectual fathers, but Lymie's father is much worse than Spud's. In examining the two families, it is obvious that the lack of any constant maternal presence in Lymie's life is one of the main causes of the difference in the two boys' trauma. Mr. Peters is damaging enough on his own, and the lack of any maternal counterpoint to his toxic behavior is ruinous. We begin to understand their families' lives when we are introduced to their respective homes. The state of each boys' houses closely mirrors the state of their family. Spud's home is unfamiliar, but it is ultimately functional. Lymie's house is a wasteland compared to Spud's. "The room was small, dark, and in considerable disorder . . . There was fluff under the bed and a fine gritty dust on everything" (Maxwell 28). Before the Peters family had a house, they were living temporarily in motels and apartments. This house presents a small semblance of stability for Lymie, but it is left disordered and uncared for. What Mr. Latham lacks as a father is covered by the presence of his wife. Neither parent can provide everything, but in many cases, they can provide enough together to raise their children healthily. The Latham family has stability not found in the Peters household primarily due to the cohabitation of both paternal and maternal forces within the family. The lack of stability in Lymie's life is apparent to Mrs. Latham, who serves as an adopted maternal presence to the boy. "That explains everything . . . I knew there was something wrong the minute I saw him" (Maxwell 80).

Lymie's family is left in deep turmoil after his mother's death. Lymie and Mr. Peters deal with the loss in separate ways. Lymie remembers his mother as a figure that provided the emotional support his father doesn't give him: "Alma, everyone called her. The richness and warmth of the sound. Alma . . . Alma . . . Like the comfort he got from leaning against her thigh" (Maxwell 91). If his mother had been around to provide him with validation and attention, Lymie would not have ended up with the trauma that nearly kills him. Mr. Peters is much less affected by the loss. "When he talked like this, it was largely to make himself suffer (he too had trouble remembering his wife's face, and the last years of his marriage had not been as happy as the first; there had been quarrels and misunderstanding, also that girl in the barber shop)" (Maxwell 91). There is an understanding from Mr. Peters that he was as bad of a husband as he is a father. He does not seek his son's sympathy for their loss because he knows he does not deserve it. He does not experience the loss as deeply as his son does. Mr. Peters is defined by his love of pleasure. The women that he covets and the alcohol that numbs him serve as two forms of pleasure that drive his actions. It is interesting that he chooses to "make himself suffer" at the memory of his wife. This willingness to forgo pleasure only exists when Mr. Peters is thinking of his wife. There is no evidence of him ever sacrificing his pleasure for Lymie throughout the novel.

The traumas both boys experience from their failed fathers are reflected during the events at Hotel Balmoral (Eliot 48-58). In an effort to enter adulthood, the boys attend a ritual that mimics pubescent maturation rituals. It is there that they attempt to enter manhood through shared humiliation and physical violence. The ritual is a complete failure for everyone involved. These young men may be mimicking the adulthood rituals that are performed around the world, but they have left out one of the most important aspects of these rituals.

All this requires the presence and active participation of grown men. Boys . . . aren't equal to it. In their hands, the rights of puberty are reduced to a hazing . . . The novices are in no way prepared to pass over into the world of maturity and be a companion to their fathers (Maxwell 57).

These boys don't know any better. Their actions have the feel of growth, but in actuality their attempts are pale shades of performative masculinity. Without their fathers, these young men are simply playing at manhood instead of properly transitioning into that stage of life.

The ritual becomes a failure, but Spud and Lymie gain quite a bit from it. It is at the ritual that Spud begins to feel responsible for Lymie. "If anything happened to the boy ahead of him, if he were hurt in any way, every son-of-a-bitch and bastard in the place would answer for it" (Maxwell 52). Throughout the novel, Spud begins to change from Lymie's friend to his protector. His previous forays into physical domination begin to morph into paternal feelings towards Lymie. Lymie's position in their relationship dynamic also changes as the novel nears its conclusion. Lymie pushes through his arrested development through his suicide attempt, which acts as a sort of rebirth for Lymie. For much of the novel, he is incapable of taking even the slightest action. This radical true first action for Lymie pushes him to a more equal level in the dynamic of his relationship with Spud. His influence in the relationship serves as a maternal presence that counteracts Spud's paternal presence. The two accept this at the end of the novel in an act similar to matrimony. "They looked at each other with complete knowledge at last, with full awareness of what they meant to each other and of all that had ever passed between them. After a moment, Spud leaned forward slowly and kissed Lymie on the mouth" (Maxwell 284). It is at this moment, and not the previous moment at the hotel, that the implicit understanding that they share accomplishes something that a group of misguided boys could never have done for them. They have synergized their own relationship with separate but equal maternal and paternal presences that provide them with the emotional and physical support that they had been missing from their ineffectual fathers.

From mid-twentieth century America, we return to England. The play *King Lear*, which was written well over two hundred years before either of the previous two works, showed the world that fatherhood could be destructive on many different levels. King Lear is the story of two aging fathers. Despite being somewhat different in rank, both men are unable to prevent their families from falling apart. These two aging fathers place their trust in the wrong children, and this leads to terrible consequences for them and the children that harbor true feelings of filial responsibility towards them. Shakespeare often made use of archetypes in his work: the uncaring father, the heroic son, the powerful wife, and the dutiful daughter. By breaking a character down into their archetypal form, we are given a thorough overview of that character's function and drives. Their wants and needs move from the personal to the universal. Shakespeare's inclusion of Gloucester, a separate father going through a journey similar to that of Lear, is another narrative tool that universalizes the subject of fatherhood in the play. The use of archetypes and parallel characters in *King Lear* will reinforce some of the basic truths about the literary presentation of fathers, their children, and the damage done when fathers fail.

King Lear is a monster of a man. He understands next to nothing, and he puts his trust in even less. He is held apart from the other fathers in this essay by both his class and his temperament. His rage, jealousy, unfairness, and need for emotional validation from his children makes him the quintessential example of the failed father archetype. Lear, at the opening of the play, embodies paternity at its most lethal. In return for raising and providing for his children, he expects his daughters to pay him back due to the filial responsibility that he thinks they owe him. Early in the play, he makes it known to his daughters that he will parcel out his kingdom based on the love that they declare they hold for him. "Tell me, my daughters/Since now we will divest us both of rule/Interest of territory, cares of State/Which of you shall we say doth love us most?" (1.1, 50-53). This power that he bestows on his daughters is mainly performative. In return for these new kingdoms, his daughters must continue to recognize him as ruler. Lear puts a lot of importance upon his position as a father. He is willing to forsake an enormous amount of social and political power based on the power that he thinks he will retain thanks to his role as their father and as the ex-regent. Lear expects his role in their relationship to supersede the role his daughters now serve as regent-princesses. Lear's need for his daughters to show their love is the beginning of his downfall. Before examining the daughter that fulfills the role of the good child, we need to examine the two daughters that serve as examples of bad children, Goneril and Regan. Lear chooses to place the kingdom in control of these two daughters that are willing to play his game. It is evident that both Regan and Goneril are paying him lip service. They ultimately do not care about their father, and instead, they say what they must so that he parcels out what they feel is owed to them. Lear slowly loses what remains of his dwindling social power when his daughters choose to turn their back on their filial responsibility. Regan, upon seeing her father begin to lose his power, does not comfort him, but instead, reminds him of his weakness. "I pray you, father, being weak, seem so" (4.4, 200). There are almost no maternal forces in this play. Despite being raised and provided for by Lear, Regan and Goneril are completely unwilling to serve as maternal forces for their father at the tail end of his life. Both women are instead primarily driven by power and success; and despite being female, they both exhibit very masculine qualities.

Regan may fill the same role as her sister, but she is not equal. Goneril is by far the biggest antagonist in Lear's family. If Lear is the quintessential failed father, then Goneril is the definitive example of a failed daughter. On some level, Lear knows that Goneril has supplanted him as the dominant power in the family's dynamic. Lear curses his daughter's feminine qualities because her masculine qualities rival his own. "Hear, nature, hear; dear Goddess, hear!/Suspend thy purpose, if thou didst intend/To make this creature fruitful/Into her womb convey sterility" (1.4, 282-285). Both daughters are willing to take care of their father, but only if he acquiesces to their new position as queen and parent. Lear is unable to accept this change in power dynamics and views the actions of his daughters as willful betrayal. The abuse of his daughters eventually drives Lear mad. In his madness, he flees into a tempest and the violence he witnesses outside allows him to gain some clarity within. It is this understanding that allows the crazed Lear to see the similarities between himself and Goneril. He compares himself to his daughter following his time in the tempest. "I know that voice/ Ha! Goneril with a white beard" (4.6, 96-97).

The slow destruction of his mental health presents us with evidence of one of Lear's most glaring character flaws: his inability to understand the emotional state of himself or his children. "I have full cause of weeping, but this heart/Shall break into a hundred thousand Flaws/Or ere I'll weep" (2.4, 283-285). Lear is defined by his anger; this anger may have served him well as king, but it gets him nowhere with his children. Nowhere is the damage caused by his temper more visible than in his betrayal of Cordelia. Cordelia fills the role of one of the only examples of the good child role in the play alongside Edgar. She is the only daughter that is truly willing to honor the filial responsibility toward Lear. Despite her feelings of true love towards her father, she is unwilling to debase herself for her inheritance at the opening of the play.

"Unhappy that I am, I cannot heave/My heart into my mouth. I love your Majesty/According to my bond, no more, nor less" (1.1, 93-95). The need to hear his daughters express their love was motivated primarily by a self-righteous pride as the leader of both his kingdom and his family. Cordelia sees the exercise for what it is, a paltry attempt for Lear to emotionally connect with his daughters on the most shallow of levels.

Cordelia's continued sense of filial obligation towards her father is indicative of her role as not only a good child, but also one of the only feminine presences in the play. Cordelia's understanding of the love between herself and Lear is more complete than any other relationship found here. The care she takes in telling her father her feelings show a level of emotional understanding that is not found in her family members. "That lord whose hand must take my plight shall carry/Half my love with him, half my care and duty/Sure I will never marry like my sisters/To love my father all" (1.1, 103-105). The difference between Lear and Cordelia's understanding of love is striking. Lear seeks a love that is surface level and will only serve him. Cordelia presents him with a true love that has limits but is ultimately free of the faults found in Goneril and Regan's love. Cordelia remains loyal to her father despite being banished from her family and her country. Her maternal instinct after finding her father further separates her role from that of her sisters. "O, my dear father, restoration hang/Thy medicine on my lips, and let this kiss/Repair those violent harms that my two sisters/Have in their reverence made" (4.7, 26-29). The care that Cordelia gives her father is not lost on Lear. It is Cordelia's steadfast love that ultimately redeems Lear and allows him to emotionally connect with someone for the first time in the play. "Be your tears wet? Yes, faith. I pray, weep not/If you have poison for me, I will drink it/I know you do not love me; for you sisters/Have, as I do remember, done me wrong/You have some cause, they have not" (4.7, 71-74). This admittance of wrongdoing on Lear's part is incredibly telling. The man from the beginning of the play would never notice another character's suffering, and he would never admit his role in that suffering. Lear is categorically bad for the majority of the play. It is only Cordelia's steadfast love through her filial obligation to her father that allows him to grow as a character and escape the hurtful archetype that he inhabits.

The dichotomy found in the roles of Lear and his children can also be found in the relationship of Gloucester and his children. Like Lear, Gloucester places his trust in the wrong child. The fallout from this decision is just as damaging as Lear's misguided decision to trust Regan and Goneril. Gloucester's sons, Edmund and Edgar, serve the same function as the daughters of Lear. Edmund serves as the uncaring child, while Edgar fills the role of the faithful child alongside Cordelia. Edmund's role as a bad character is exacerbated by the circumstances of his birth. "His breeding, sir, hath been at my charge: I have so often blushed to acknowledge him, that now I am brazed to it" (1.1, 10-11). Edmund's existence as a bastard informs every action that he takes. Despite having his father's love and favor, he knows that eventually he will be pushed aside due to his brother's natural birth. The knowledge that everything will be left to his brother is the thought that pushes him to manipulate his family. "Wherefore should I/Stand in the plague of custom, and permit/The curiosities of nations to deprive me" (1.2, 1-3). Edmund is not driven by love; instead, he is driven by his need for power. In this he is extraordinarily similar to Regan and Goneril. Edmund stands alongside Dunstan and Godfrey Cass as one of the only examples of a failed son among the three works covered in this essay.

If Edmund is an example of the failed son, then Edgar is squarely placed in the successful son category. Edgar constantly shows that his faith and respect for his father never wavers. This is difficult for Edgar as his father repeatedly falls for Edmund's deceptions.

Gloucester never fails Edmund. He awards Edmund the same love and respect as his own natural son. The failure in their relationship falls squarely on Edmund, who denies his own filial obligation in the search for power. The only son that Gloucester actively fails is Edgar. Gloucester's misguided belief in Edmund mirrors Lear's trust in his daughters' expressions of love. Each act only serves as a deception through which the children can take power from their fathers and gain control of their dominant role in the relationship. Edgar's actions as a faithful son are eventually validated when he overhears his father discuss his son's plight. "I am almost mad myself. I had a son/Now outlawed from my blood; he sought my life/But lately, very late. I loved him, friend/No father his son dearer. True to tell thee" (3.4, 169-172). Edgar eventually saves his father in a manner similar to Cordelia's rescue of Lear. After tricking Gloucester into thinking he jumped off a cliff, Edgar is present for the metaphorical rebirth of his father. It is only through Edgar's constant love and paternal presence that Gloucester is relieved from the wickedness of his blindness. Gloucester is so overcome with shock and joy from his son's re-appearance that it kills him. The families of Gloucester and Lear mirror each other closely. Both Lear and Gloucester are reduced to shadows of their former selves due to the betrayal of their children. For both men it is ultimately the love of their children that pulls them back from the broken state that they linger in for the majority of the play.

The presence of a character from a different social stratum is important for this work. The lives of kings and their families are so far removed from the comprehension of many. By presenting Gloucester, who is much easier to understand than the unreachable Lear, everyone, be they prince or pauper, can find common ground in the discussion of fatherhood and its failure. The fact that both children who are betrayed ultimately serve as the instigator for their fathers' salvation is another lesson of great importance.

Fathers may fail, but it does not have to serve as a debilitating source of personal failure for their children. We do not have to be defined by the failures of our fathers. Like anything else that is detrimental in life, failed fatherhood can be overcome by those that survive it.

I have put a lot of thought into whether good fatherhood is possible. I think that it is possible for men to be good fathers if they try hard enough. Whether that fatherhood is successful without the presence of a maternal force, I am less certain. My own father failed spectacularly at paternity. The beatings he would inflict upon my mother and I have left a deep trauma that in many ways defines the people that we are today. Regardless of how we have processed that trauma, the abuse and failure of my father has become the proverbial millstone around the neck of two generations in my family. I wrote this essay as a mental exercise to try to understand the importance of fatherhood. I find it hard to place any importance upon fathers, as the mothers in my life were the ones who stepped up and made me the man I am today. The feelings of awe and love that most owe to their father do not exist for me. When I think of mine, the only word that is appropriate is damage. Of course, I forgive my father; if I have learned anything from the women who raised me, it is how to be a better man than he ever was.

Above all things, fatherhood is complex. I wonder if I know enough about failure from my father to not make the same mistakes when I have children. I fear that the trauma he has caused will carry on, damaging my experience as a father like Squire Cass and Godfrey. Living in your father's shadow is something that is part and parcel of life for every Chicano man. I accept this as well as I can, but I still worry that the shadow cast by my father will darken my childrens' lives as well.

This essay has shown me that it is possible for children to get out from underneath damaging relationships with their fathers. Writing this has taught me that any man is capable of being a father, but the implementation of good fatherhood is determined by the individual.

If great men like King Lear can fail as fathers, then what chance did my father ever stand? I would rather treat my children like Silas Marner did. If being a good father means becoming a member of that old, disinherited race, then count me in.

Bibliography

Eliot, George. Silas Marner. Strand, London: Penguin Books, 1996.
Maxwell, William. The Folded Leaf. New York: Random House, 1996.
Shakespeare, William. King Lear. New York: Penguin Group, 1996.

Unfair Education in a "Fair" Country
Rodney (Lucas) McNatt

In the late 19th to 20th centuries, the United States was considered to be at the top of the world in terms of having the leading educational system. Since then, times have changed, and so have other countries and their efforts to adapt to a more modern style of teaching. This has caused some nations to either outrank the United States or head in that direction if they haven't done so already. More specifically, at the international level, why is it that some states within the nation are excelling at public education, while others are left defunded and in the shadows? In the duration of this essay, I will speak about how our country as a whole is depriving many children of a proper education. The reason is not in order to become the leading world educator, but to resolve the issue as to why many individual states are worse off than others, especially due to the fact that if every citizen is offered the right to a free education, then they should have the same opportunity even across state lines. We will look into this by speaking about my own personal experience from being raised in one of the lowest-rated states in terms of education, evaluating statistical data of rankings by state, financial differences, and by reviewing the main problems within the school system as a whole.

New Mexico vs. the U.S.

Growing up in New Mexico, I found it to be quite a unique experience that people from other places do not always get to see or go through every day. It has a very rich culture, especially with the opportunity of growing up in the capital city of Santa Fe. The oldest state capital in the country has very influential Native as well as Hispanic roots. It gifted me with becoming a more cultured individual, and I appreciate the backgrounds of all people. My sphere of influence was broad and rather refreshing in my opinion; but in terms of education, it actually became quite the opposite.

In my own eyes, our educational system should be seen by many as a rather alarming nightmare. As a child, you are unaware and unable to understand that most states and regions have different curricula, or foundations by which they teach their students. If you were a parent, or if you are one now, how do you determine where the best place is to enroll your child in order for them to receive a proper education? Even if the school has the best overall grade in the city or county, is it the best in the state? Let's say that is the scenario. The next question would be: does the state have the best rankings of public education within the country? Or is it at least one of the top ten states? If not, private school is an option, but many families cannot afford it. I know my family couldn't. Finally, you can always move to another state, but as you might expect, this would mean you would have to quit your job, find a new one (same for your spouse), and leave friends and family behind. But why must a family go through such various and extreme measures in order to give their child a proper education?

It was not until I had reached my high school years that I paid attention to how other states ran their education systems (which seems kind of obvious, I mean how many kids do you know actually look up that sort of thing?). It came to my attention from the complaints of my teachers and their fellow staff members. Their tempers habitually flared whenever we would have mandatory statewide testing, which threw plans off the rails for teachers who had certain learning objectives planned for each week throughout the semester. But how exactly does our curriculum or system in New Mexico compare to other states within the country? To understand this, we must refer to the statistical data provided.

DATA AND EVIDENCE

Before looking further into data charts and evidence, I bring up New Mexico as the main subject in this paper for many reasons: (A) I grew up here and have been educated in the state from preschool to now being a junior in college. Therefore, I consider myself an expert in any in-state issues. (B) Even though many of you did not grow up here, you may not have had the best education yourselves growing up, and many might not even realize it, so, I am spreading awareness to you as well. (C) Many of my students and peers from Western New Mexico University are on campus, or within state lines (via online), so they might be able to understand where I am coming from if they are in the Silver City area. Thus, I've tried to make this topic as relatable as possible to my fellow classmates, regardless of where they are from.

Now, in order to evaluate data, much of our evidence will come from the work of financial writer Adam McCann and his article from WalletHub, "States with the Best and Worst School Systems", who extends upon specific classifications, rankings, individual issues, and methodologies regarding the nation's education. His main findings were as follows: All fifty states, including the District of Columbia (Washington D.C.), were evaluated in two separate categories, and then later received an overall total score that was based on a 100-point scale. The two main categories were "Quality" and "Safety." At the bottom of this list, ranked 51 out of 51 results, was New Mexico (which I was already anticipating before reading, just due to feedback received from teachers and other educators throughout my life). The state's safety rank hit a 49, while the quality rank was an overall 51. Leading for a total score out of 100, to sum up to an astounding 27.61. Other key ideas to point out on this chart are those states that are next to each other on the ranking list (i.e., if they are close in ranking, being 10th, 11th, and 12th) have little separation in points from each other, only being above or behind the next state by no more than 1-3 points at a time. After evaluating the results in New Mexico, I found that we are as far as 7.4 points behind the closest state, which for reference, is #50 Louisiana which holds a rank of 34.65. Since we are on the subject, New Mexico's dropout rates are tied for 50th place and has hit this number constantly in its math and reading scores. For comparison, and overall curiosity, the leading state in public education is Massachusetts, with a total score of 71.73, with both quality and safety ranks placing 1st. Do keep in mind that just because it says "number one" under the state's name, this is out of a 100-point scale. Any person who went to school, regardless of how good your school was, knows that this score is a C+ on any test or essay. Also, when we see how well a state such as Massachusetts is doing when compared to New Mexico, or even Louisiana, we realize that there is, in fact, a clear educational divide, so why can't we all average at least an 80 or above on these data records? The next point to follow can quite possibly be the answer for some of our own issues, if applied correctly and efficiently.

NEXT School

To learn more about how our system is damaged and simply outdated, we can investigate the findings and research of R.Z. Shah Trust, who has formed NEXT school. For those unfamiliar with NEXT, it is "a revolutionary international school in Mulund, Mumbai. [It is] India's first Big Picture School. By putting students at the center of their own learning [they] aim to make education more engaging and relevant" in the modern era (Shah Trust, Next School). Roughly four years ago, NEXT put out a video titled, "6 Problems with our School System." We will now briefly study and explain each of these problems, as they go over the old systems of education that are still in place today.

The first of these problems, with ours and most other school systems, is the "Industrial Age Values." The school atmosphere we are surrounded by today is based on what was established over 100 years ago when we were amid the biggest industrial boom the economy has ever seen. Schools were designed to get children into the habit of being factory workers on assembly lines, if you can imagine (if not, refer to the video that will be displayed in the sources section). In school, you sit in rows at your desk, and everyone follows instructions. If the teacher says, "flip to page 43," you flip to page 43. If they say to "finish an assignment by the end of class," you do so, or at least try to. The ideal theory was to create an atmosphere of following rather than leading. The second subject our school systems value is theorized by NEXT as a "lack of autonomy." One of the main benefits of having a job today that was unavailable years ago, or even having the ability to study or work from home, is that you can manage your time in whichever way you choose. You can work when you want and utilize media and sites as resources. In the school setting, time is managed for you, and you do not have the ability to take charge of your own life. You have a set schedule of when to study, when to take your break (recess), and even simple activities such as reading are limited to a specific time span before writing about the material. Lastly, if the school were to tell you to move on from fourth to fifth grade, you would do exactly that, regardless of whether you felt the need to stay behind due to whether or not you accumulated all necessary information. The third point brought up in this video is that "Inauthentic Learning" is a major issue. School systems believe that everyone must learn the given pieces of material in a specific way. Test scores are the main concern for this topic. As we end up learning about material throughout the course of a year, we end up trying to cram as much of the information into one final exam. Oftentimes (which is mostly every time), the instructors are forced to remove much material from the test due to how many questions are on it, or because there is a time limit included. Now, let's be honest here, as a student, how effective are tests after you pass it? Ask yourself, after hours of studying for one exam, how much of that information stayed with you throughout the years? Could you recall it if it was raised in a discussion or debate? I'm assuming few of you can remember the answer to your final essay question that you wrote for the history exam when you were a junior in high school. The fourth theory (or fact, in my opinion) is that there is "No Passion or Interest" that fits the needs of everyone within our outdated system. Everyone is taught the same way, as previously stated. This means that no one can develop their own personal interests or passions if they are not majoring in one of the core curriculum's classes in college. Now I will say, to focus on every need of an individual is a tough task, but in a different system, this could be achievable to some extent. In order for any individual to succeed in life, it is highly relied upon their passion. Passion makes one feel as though they are contributing to society in a truly beneficial way, rather than being similar or "basic" to everyone around them. The fifth problem stated is "How We Learn as Individuals." No two people are the same, and as a result, we don't learn the same way either. Furthermore, we don't always learn something at the same speed. Some of us are quick learners in certain areas and/ or topics. For example, I play college football. If it takes me two weeks to learn the entirety of a team's playbook, and I am able to compete in a game right afterwards without any mental errors, would I expect the same results from someone who has never read a playbook or even touched a football in their entire life? Of course not. So, why does it apply to our school systems? If someone is forced to repeat a grade due to a lack of success in the time frame of one school year, they are referred to by many as failures. Even the name says so: "you have failed the fourth grade." Or vice versa: they may have passed the class, but still don't know all the material needed for the subsequent grade level (as stated earlier in the paper). This puts them in a tough position for the following year. The last problem within our school system is "Lecturing." Some teaching professionals do it, and some do not. Either way, we have all been exposed to it at some point. This tactic is dehumanizing due to the lack of interaction available during these lessons. We are an interactive species, yet we cannot communicate for an hour and a half about material we are forced to learn about. This leads to confused kids who are behind in school. Conversely, students that are ahead in class are often bored because they have to sit through a lecture they could basically teach themselves, which leads to an unmotivated and a rather lazy outcome.

FINANCES

The school systems in our country are unfair and disproportionate, the main reasons being financial struggles that some states go through, and the fact that they lack the resources which others may have. Funding is distributed differently from state to state, therefore, the main question concerns funding itself. As stated by the ASCD authors of the Research Synthesis / Unequal School Funding in the United States, Bruce Biddle and David Berliner state that "Nearly half of the funding for public schools in the United States, however, is provided through local taxes, generating large differences in funding between wealthy and impoverished communities" (National Center for Education Statistics, 2000) (Bruce J. Biddle and David C. Berliner, ASCD). There are a total of three main influences across every state that help provide for Public Education. These providers come from Federal, State, and Local governments. Sources from the U.S. Department of Education has shown us that State and Local governments contribute roughly the same amounts (money-wise) to their schools. Federal money contributions provide the smallest shares (which makes sense, as we learn in the reading that public schools are state funded). The research has also shown us that schools with higher rankings contribute in other outside manners, including resident taxes. Not all states do this, and quite honestly, it shows that states who only rely on a few sources of funding do not succeed, and the following results, as far as ranking goes, should not be surprising.

To find the reasoning for such funding issues that vary state-by-state, we refer yet again to Bruce Biddle and David Berliner's input, which narrows the reasoning down to three main categories. Situation 1, history: "Initially, schools were often financed by voluntary contributions . . . [at] the end of the 19th century the tradition of funding them through local property taxes was widespread. This tradition had real advantages because many families were living in small, relatively isolated communities with similar standards of living . . . As time passed, fewer people lived in such communities. Instead, more people crowded into major cities . . . [some even] moved to the suburbs . . . As the suburbs grew, the inhabitants retained the tradition of funding public schools through local property taxes, but now this system is flawed. Parents who moved to affluent suburbs were generally willing to fund well-equipped, well-staffed public schools for their own children" (Bruce J. Biddle and David C. Berliner, ASCD). With this, we can piece together that citizens in urban and suburban areas saw no use in providing funds to schools their children were not attending. This left educational institutions that were underpopulated and in rural communities out to dry with the little community funding they had. Situation 2, "Beliefs About the Causes of Poverty": different ideologies. Individualism holds that success and failure result mainly from individual effort rather than social circumstance. This leads to the blame of individuals failing due to the lack of their own efforts. Essentialism claims that less privileged groups (such as African Americans, Hispanics, Native Americans, or women) inherit genetic characteristics that account for whatever lack of successes they have experienced. The culture of Poverty Thesis argues that minority persons fail because of inappropriate traditions in the subcultures of their homes, communities, or ethnic groups (see Moynihan, 1969). (Bruce J. Biddle and David C. Berliner, ASCD).

I believe that Biddle and Berliner are spot-on when stating that "Each of these belief systems can lead to the argument that because students from impoverished homes are unlikely to benefit from a "quality" education, funding public schools equally in rich and poor neighborhoods would only waste tax dollars" (Bruce J. Biddle and David C. Berliner, ASCD). The third and final situation is "Flawed Studies": "Reluctance to provide equal funds for U.S. public schools has also been fueled by claims from prominent researchers, reviewers, and others asserting that the level of funding for schools does not affect student achievement. Not surprisingly, such claims often come from sources [such as the Heritage Foundation (1989)] that are traditionally hostile to public education" (Bruce J. Biddle and David C. Berliner, ASCD). I see here a pattern of many societal and racial prejudices that come into play with how states, the government, and the citizens within it treat our educational systems. This is alarming and rather disturbing as we are supposed to be one united nation.

TRACING BACK TO THE LOCAL SITUATION

To get back on the topic of New Mexico education, we refer to Elizabeth Miller, from the *Bitterroot* newsletter, as she writes about the hardships and struggles that one individual had to experience throughout her time in public school. Michelle Soto, in 2009, attended fourth grade in Albuquerque, NM. She was a non-native English speaker, and primarily spoke Spanish. The article stated that her teacher had no idea as to what to do with her and would just let her play games throughout the day as the lessons were being taught. She then got passed on to the fifth grade, where it claims that by this time, she was "bullied by her classmates for not knowing how to speak English. At home, she would cry to her mom and say she didn't want to go to school" (Miller, *Bitterroot*). This was not the only case or occurrence in which a similar situation like this has happened within the state of New Mexico. "In 2014, dozens of families and six school districts sued the state of New Mexico's Public Education Department for failing to provide for the needs of all its students ... A 2008 report commissioned by New Mexico's legislature found its education system underfunded by nearly $335 million" (Miller, *Bitterroot*). Although this is sad information to read, I do find myself facing a level of sanity after reading, because it tells me that I am not the only one who realizes the odds are stacked against New Mexico school attendees. I can also relate with the kids that are similar to Michelle. Although I knew English, I have seen the exact same situation occur in my own schools, even reaching as far as high school.

POTENTIAL SOLUTIONS

So, what can change? This is a difficult question for many; it was for me at the beginning of this paper. But after extensive research, my suggested solutions are quite simple, and/or attainable. Solution one: quit continuing to place children through the traditional learning system that was established from previous centuries. Take systems, and even input from other countries, as well as "new age" school systems such as NEXT, and figure out ways to apply different items to create the best environment for a true learning experience. Solution two: get people to care. If you might notice in the data chart that will be provided below, states that don't have many big cities or major urban populations suffer in funding for their schools. If citizens realized the immediate and long-term effects that it has on the entire country's outcome of education, more people would be willing to distribute their wealth. Solution three: Find more resources other than local payments. Whenever you see a candidate running for president, if you hear them talking about "taking on education," the reality is that there is not much that they can actually do to achieve progress. This is due to the fact that states hold the primary funding source in education. I believe with a more reliable source, and potentially more tax dollars that will be directed to education, we can make true change. My final solution: Start at square one. There is no need to make a final decision and apply it to every school in the nation right away. Samples done in small areas in the lowest-rated states or counties will give us an impression of whether or not a new plan is effective. Based on what I have written out for you today, I do not think that New Mexico is a bad place to start these test trials. In the meantime, look out and be aware of what type of education your child is truly getting. Take into account that there are many ways that we as citizens can create a better future school system.

Sources

Adam McCann, Financial Writer, "States with the Best & Worst School Systems", WalletHub, Juyl 27, 2020. July 27, 2020. https://wallethub.com/edu/e/states-with-the-best-schools/5335

NEXT School website and database, R.Z. Shah Trust. https://www.nextschool.org/

"6 Problems with our school system", NEXT School, Dec. 16th, 2016. https://www.youtube.com/watch?v=okpg-lVWLbE

New Mexico Failed Its Students. Now the State is Rethinking Public Education, Elizabeth Miller, Bitterroot, May 17, 2019. https://bitterrootmag.com/2019/05/17/after-historic-lawsuit-new-mexico-begins-an-inclusive-education-overhaul/

A Research Synthesis / Unequal School Funding in the United States, Bruce J. Biddle and David C. Berliner, ASCD Educational Leadership, May 2002. http://www.ascd.org/publications/educational-leadership/may02/vol59/num08/Unequal-School-Funding-in-the-United-States.aspx#:~:text=Public%20school%20funding%20in%20the,between%20wealthy%20and%20impoverished%20communities.

Code-Switching in the English-learning Classroom: Beneficial or Obstructive?

Melanie Woods-Sedillo

Though long thought to be an abhorrent obstruction to language learning, code-switching is gaining traction as well as a better perception in recent years. Code-switching (CS) is defined as the process of shifting from one language or dialect to another. This is especially common in people who are learning an additional language. In more recent years, code-switching is being found to be very beneficial, at both the academic and social levels, for native Spanish-speaking students who are learning English. While historically the research has shown the opposite, it is being discovered that the conditions the research on code-switching were done under were not ideal to properly quantify the scope of benefits. Previous research on code-switching has focused primarily on deficits, but these deficits can be explained by far more than a simple language difference. Not only is there a difference in the language that is spoken between a native English speaker and an English learner, but there are cultural and religious differences as well that contribute to the patterns of English language learners and a perceived deficit. It may not be (and often isn't) cognitive at all, but simply a difference in understandings due to cultural differences. This paper will explore the different ideologies regarding code-switching as well as its benefits.

It has often been thought throughout time that code-switching gives students less practice in the target language. It is even quite often seen as a lazy way to approach language learning. It is commonly seen as blasphemous when mixing the native language with the target language in the same sentence. There are many people including parents, teachers, and school administrators who have these beliefs. Some say that because the brain has to "switch" back and forth between languages, that the act harms any progress in the target language because too much time is spent "translating" within the brain. This belief in particular ignores the fact that in learning a language, one is already translating their thoughts from the native language to the target language. This belief is one based in ignorance. It is most often thought to be true by those who are monolingual because they do not and cannot understand how the brain learns a second (or third, or fourth …) language, unless they begin to learn a language themselves. Margarita Hidalgo made a great point in her 1988 paper that has stayed relevant over 30 years later: "Intrasentential code-switching, however, can be perceived by those who are monolingual as an abrupt, inexplicable, and often annoying change of languages. For decades I had observed that Mexican residents of Juarez reacted negatively to this 'otherwise natural' style of communications." (Hidalgo, 1988, p. 2). This shows that negative attitudes towards linguistic code-switching comes from both monolingual English speakers as well as monolingual Spanish speakers. However, as "Spanglish" and code-switching more commonly occur in the United States, it is primarily monolingual Americans who are the most vocal about their dislike of the two.

The ignorance of modern, monolingual English-speaking Americans is derived from decades of racist rhetoric, policies, and mindsets in the United States. The U.S. is one of the most diverse countries, yet also one of the most racist and ignorant – especially when it comes to language. This has led to a myriad of issues for speakers of languages other than English. In an article from the *Bilingual Research Journal*, it is stated that: "Critics, however, claim that the simultaneous use of two languages signals linguistic interference or evidence of insufficient development of a person's full linguistic repertoire (Baker, 2006).

Often, these criticisms derive from a political and colonial past in which nationalism and patriotism are linked to the use of language (Mazak, 2017).

Socially constructed language hierarchies emanate from unequal power conditions and unwarranted societal preferences rather than any empirically provable linguistic superiority (Shin, 2017). The perceived prestige and symbolic power of certain language varieties results in a form of linguistic imperialism that privileges some languages at the expense, and possible peril, of others" (Hopewell & Abril-Gonzalez, 2019). This so-called "patriotism" fuels the fire of negative opinions regarding second languages and code-switching. It has led to the development of fear in students who are learning English, as this attitude implies that the home language is somehow inferior to the target language and needs to be pushed aside for the success of the target language. This is unfair and unequitable to our emergent bilinguals; luckily, more research is coming about that is showing exactly how wrong these attitudes are.

Furthermore, these attitudes seem to become internalized within the emergent bilinguals. In their article in the *Journal of Multilingual and Multiculture Development*, Dewaele and Wei mention that "Languages are best kept separate and well-formed according to tightly defined monolingual rules. Even bilinguals who code-switch themselves sometimes believe that CS is an indication of laziness or poor linguistic proficiency" (Dewaele & Wei, 2014). This purist ideology only results in hindering the learning and success of emergent bilinguals. They will begin to think of themselves as dumb, lazy, or unable to "properly" learn a language. Students learn best in environments where they are comfortable and encouraged. If there is a prevailing ideology around them that suggests that code-switching is anything but positive, the student will begin to doubt themselves and slow their progress. The same paper states that "CS in language teaching has seldom been seen as a facilitating strategy. Instead, it is regarded as a sign of lack of proficiency in the target language. Likewise, CS in young children is often taken as an example of poor cognitive control or lack of sensitivity of the appropriate choice of language" (Dewaele & Wei, 2014). Parents often share these views about code-switching, as shown here: "Parents in particular are concerned that CS may confuse children as they develop their knowledge and skills in different languages" (Dewaele & Wei, 2014). These ideologies have prevailed for an indeterminate amount of time, and only serve to hinder the natural process of second language acquisition in students.

Fortunately, there has been advancements in research recently in regard to code-switching, the effect that it has on language acquisition, and the benefits to be had when using code-switching in the classroom. A great point made in Dewaele and Wei's article is as follows: "However, recent research in bilingual and multilingual education has provided evidence that CS can not only be used as an effective pedagogical strategy for teaching and learning but also should be seen as a sign of linguistic creativity and criticality. Some researchers in bilingual and multilingual first language acquisition have argued that CS is evidence of advanced executive control whereby the child justifies his or her language choice to manage the communicative demand" (2014). This is the complete opposite of the ideologies covered above. Rather than being a hindrance or an obstruction to learning a target language, research is beginning to prove that it is actually of benefit to an emergent bilingual to code-switch, especially within the classroom.

Dewaele and Wei later state that "Their arguments have been backed up by extensive linguistic analyses of the complex structures of CS which suggest that the ability to switch between languages in conversational interaction requires high linguistic knowledge as well as sociolinguistic sensitivities" (2014). The fact that research is showing that code-switching is not only beneficial but evident of linguistic knowledge shows that the students have a better grasp on the language that they are learning than they are given credit for. Code-switching doesn't occur for lack of cognition, but for lack of a manner of expressing something in the target language. In this way, code-switching is thought to be a resource rather than a hindrance, and it is very beneficial to the student's progress.

Another study that shows the benefits of bilingualism and code-switching is called Two is better than one: bilingual education promotes the flexible mind. The discussion portion of the study states that "The present study indicates that an intensive bilingual language context is associated with a flexible mind and a relative focused 'scope' of attention" (Christoffels, et al., 2014, p. 6). This shows that switching between languages improves cognitive control and mental flexibility. It also improves the scope of attention in that the bilingual person is better able to focus their attention on necessary information and tune out the unnecessary. "The current results may offer some support for the idea that bilingualism promotes cognitive flexibility in general" (Christoffels, et al., 2014, p. 7). This study also found that the bilingual group was associated with lower residual switch costs than their nonbilingual counterparts. These results promote the use of code-switching in the classroom, because of the multiple benefits seen in those who switch between languages on a frequent daily basis.

These benefits are seen both within a school setting and outside of it. Given some of the results of the study, the authors "speculate that bilingual education may induce particular cognitive-control strategies that generalize to situations that have no bearing on bilingual skills" (Christoffels, et al., 2014, p. 11). The ability to keep two or more languages separate shows both mental flexibility and focus of attention, in that there were reduced switching costs when moving from one task to another (Christoffels, et al., 2014, p. 11). This is useful in the academic setting in that the student is better able to use a flexible thinking style with less processing time. It also helps the student to ascertain unnecessary and necessary information to complete a goal more quickly (Christoffels, et al., 2014, p. 11). Christoffels, et al. do note, however, that language immersion programs do not produce the same results. Therefore, a bilingual environment where both languages are consistently exchanged is necessary in order to enjoy the benefits.

Other studies have focused on language performance within environments where code-switching is common. There are obvious benefits to being able to code-switch between a native language and a target language when learning a language. One such study by Kaushanskaya and Crespo called "Does Exposure to Code-Switching Influence Language Performance in Bilingual Children" states that "Being able to code-switch enables bilinguals to precisely express the intended meanings and to circumvent lexical gaps" (p. 1). They go on to say on the same page that the benefits of code-switching actually outweigh any processing costs that are associated with switching languages. This is particularly useful in learning a new language because it helps the student to grasp the full intended meaning by using their native language as prior knowledge to help retain the new knowledge. They also found that exposure to code-switching does not carry any risks, as some would believe, and rather can be beneficial.

Code-switching is often quite an unconscious behavior, especially in children. They use code-switching as a way to find deeper meaning in their new language as well as new ways to express themselves and what they're feeling. In a study called "Voluntary Language Switching in English-Spanish Bilingual Children" by Gross and Kaushanskaya, they point out that "many bilingual individuals engage in code-switching when conversing with other bilingual speakers; they switch back and forth between their two languages, often within the same sentence" (Gross & Kaushanskaya, 2015). It is also discussed that "as early as age two, children are able to adjust their relative use of one language or the other based on their conversation partner, although they do sometimes produce words in the inappropriate language for a given listener" (Gross & Kaushanskaya, 2015). This suggests that language switching is natural and innate, as even the youngest of dual language speakers tend to code-switch. There is evidence that "bilingual children tend to exhibit distributed linguistic knowledge, such that there are some concepts and structures they know only in Language A and others they know only in Language B" (Gross & Kaushanskaya, 2015). This suggests that the reason for code-switching lies in the lexical accessibility in one language or another. If a child cannot accurately convey the message they want to convey, they voluntarily switch to the language where they can access the expression that they want to achieve in order to properly convey the desired message.

This study by Gross and Kaushanskaya was performed "in a research laboratory or in a quiet room at home" (2015). In the discussion portion of the study, their results showed that children exhibit no switching costs in regards to accuracy when they engage in voluntary language switching (Gross & Kaushanskaya, 2015). This shows that children switch languages for accuracy and do not switch languages when it would come at a cost in accuracy. This information further supports the idea that bilingual code-switching is beneficial in children in a myriad of ways. This points to the lexical accessibility of desired expression in dual language speakers. The bilingual speakers would not switch languages if they did not have the ability to better express themselves by switching.

It is natural to switch languages when a person speaks more than one language. According to Hopewell and Abril-Gonzalez's study "Por Que Estamos Code-Switching? Understanding Language Use in a Second-Grade Classroom", they state that "The spontaneous use of two languages within a single utterance or across a series of utterances is a natural phenomenon in bilingual communities" (2019). They also point out that previous research has shown that language switching is rule governed as well as systematic, and that code-switching serves a specific purpose; it has also been found that code-switching shows language proficiency in multilingual speakers (Hopewell & Abril-Gonzalez, 2019, p. 1). Another great point mentioned in this study is that bilingual learners who are taught in bilingual environments do as well as or better than their monolingual and bilingual counterparts who are taught in English-only environments. The authors show that they understand the intricacies of bilingual individuals and the way they use their languages based on the need at the current point in time.

The authors also point out that in a lot of bilingual schools, there is an insistence upon keeping the two languages separate. This insistence ignores the evidence that using background prior knowledge in one language can help the bilingual learner to better understand and retain the course materials and target language. Teachers in a bilingual learning environment "have the opportunity to reduce a student's learning burden by attending to systematic patterns and analogies within the second language, and by pointing out connections between the second language and the first" (Hopewell & Abril-Gonzalez, 2019, p. 4-5). Rather than forcing students to only learn in and about one language at a time, allowing the students to use both languages to facilitate their own learning can greatly improve their proficiency in both languages as well as the course materials. A teacher discussed in the study uses both English and Spanish in an explicit manner, explaining when she is going to use each language and why. She has a recitation with her students: "Por qué estamos code-switching?" and the students will respond "Because we're bilingual!" (Hopewell & Abril-Gonzalez, 2019, p. 5). This fosters the positive attitude around code-switching that is so crucial towards the development of bilingualism in the classroom.

Within the bilingual classroom mentioned above, the teacher allows for humor and other forms of engagement within units. She allows the students to speak to one another in their dominant language, so long as they're still attempting the assignment in English. (Hopewell & Abril-Gonzalez, 2019, p. 10). Often, the students will use Spanish to cause an interruption that enables them to say what they want to say in English. The students consistently called their teacher "maestra" which in Spanish has deep respect and cultural meaning that is lost in English. When a student calls their teacher "teacher" in English, it is often seen as a sign of disrespect because of the cultural differences (Hopewell & Abril-Gonzalez, 2019, p. 10). This is another key point to bear in mind as educators of English language learners. There is not only a language difference to work around, but a cultural one as well. Understanding these cultural differences can help to create more engagement and motivation in the classroom, which in turn leads to success for the students. There is an article that is of particular significance regarding the benefits of code-switching in the classroom. It is called "Code-Switching Among Bilingual and Limited English Proficient Students: Possible Indicators of Giftedness" by Hughes et al., and it mentions that "In order to code-switch effectively, students must possess a high level of understanding of the 2 cultures, as well as a deep understanding of the underlying structures and purposes of 2 language systems. Code-switching, rather than reflecting the traditional view of a disadvantaged and semiliterate background, actually reflects an intellectual advantage [emphasis added]" (Hughes et al., 2006, p. 1). However, as code-switching has been commonly seen as a negative trait by schools and teachers (and even the majority culture), there is a large bias against code-switching. According to the authors, though, code-switching is "rarely a sign of confusion or inadequacy, even in very young children" (Hughes et al., 2006, p. 14). Again, we are reminded of Hopewell's comments that these biases stem from a false sense of ethnic superiority rather than an actual deficit in language.

Code-switching allows for a level of mental flexibility that isn't seen in monolinguals. According to Hughes et al., "Code switching, rather than reflecting the traditional view of a disadvantaged and semiliterate background, reflects an intellectual advantage to many students. Culturally different students who are trying to integrate two cultural systems may have greater cognitive and social flexibility" (Hughes et al., 2006, p. 18). This shows that rather than causing a deficit, that code-switching in bilingualism has effects that can influence proficiency. "…Canadian bilingual children performed better than their matched monolingual peers on all verbal IQ test scores. This seminal study overturned earlier notions that bilingual children were cognitively disadvantaged" (Hughes et al., 2006, p. 20). The study states that because of the biases and ignorant notions of the past, minority and bilingual students are not often even considered for gifted education, putting some at a disadvantage. They go on to state that "If teachers were to recognize the expressive power of code-switching and understand the sophisticated linguistic knowledge required to effectively combine two languages for a social purpose, their prejudiced beliefs about the practice, the students, and students' possible need for gifted programming may improve. Students should not be kept out of the gifted identification process or programming because of their use of sophisticated linguistic abilities that teachers may not understand nor approve of" (Hughes et al., 2006, p. 22).

All in all, it has been shown throughout the course of this paper, as well as within all of the sources listed, that there are highly polarized views about bilingual education and the role that code-switching plays in learning, proficiency, and classroom success. What sticks out the most is that every study was able to show the mental and cognitive flexibility that bilingual people show over their monolingual peers. If children are allowed to continue using these tools and expanding their knowledge of the world through two languages, their success could be immeasurable. Code-switching in the classroom serves as a tool to further understanding, retainment, and engagement in what is being learned, whether that is a target language or classroom content.

References

Christoffels, I. K., de Haan, A. M., Steenbergen, L., van den Wildenberg, W. P., & Colzato, L. S. (2015). Two is better than one: bilingual education promotes the flexible mind. Psychological research, 79(3), 371–379. https://doi.org/10.1007/s00426-014-0575-3 https://pubmed.ncbi.nlm.nih.gov/24849283/

Dewaele, J.M. & Wei, L. (2014) Attitudes towards code-switching among adult mono- and multilingual language users, Journal of Multilingual and Multicultural Development, 35:3, 235-251, https://doi.org/10.1080/01434632.2013.859687

Gross, M., Kaushanskaya, M. (2015). Voluntary language switching in English-Spanish bilingual children. Journal of Cognitive Psychology (Hove, England), 27(8), 992-1013. https://www.ncbi.nlm.nih.gov/pmc/articles/PMC4753071/

Hopewell, S. & Abril-Gonzalez, P. (2019) ¿Por qué estamos code-switching? Understanding language use in a second-grade classroom. Bilingual Research Journal, 42(1), 105-120. https://doi.org/10.1080/15235882.2018.1561554

Hidalgo, Margarita. "Perceptions of Spanish-English Code-Switching in Juarez, Mexico." (1988). https://digitalrepository.unm.edu/laii_research/14

Hughes, C., Shaunessy, E., Brice, A., Ratliff, M., McHatton, P. (2006). Code-Switching Among Bilingual and Limited English Proficient Students: Possible Indicators of Giftedness. Journal for the Education of the Gifted,100(1), 7–28. https://files.eric.ed.gov/fulltext/EJ750758.pdf

Kaushanskaya, M. & Crespo, K. (2019). Does Exposure to Code-Switching Influence Language Performance in Bilingual Children? Society for Research in Child Development, 90(3), 708-718. https://doi.org/10.1111/cdev.13235

RESEARCH

Affect, Personality, Sexism, and the Menstruating Woman

Emma Jefferson Po-sen Chu

Some researchers suggest that ambivalent sexism, affect, and personality are associated with people's attitudes towards and perceptions of menstruating women. Previous research has demonstrated that people hold negative and hostile sexist attitudes towards women who are menstruating, and that certain Big Five personality traits are correlated with people's levels of sexism. Further, researchers have found that higher benevolent sexism scores are associated with positive yet restricting emotions towards menstruating women. Therefore, it was the interest of this study to determine whether ambivalent sexist beliefs and certain personality traits can cause people to perceive women's affect more negatively when menstruation is made salient. We hypothesized that participants who viewed a menstruating woman's profile would rate her emotions as more negative than those who viewed the profile of a woman whose menstruation status was not made salient. We also hypothesized that the higher the participants' ambivalent sexism and neuroticism, the higher their perception of negative emotions in the menstruating woman. Participants (n = 85) completed measures of ambivalent sexism and Big Five personality traits on an online questionnaire. They were then randomly assigned to one of two groups where they viewed a patient profile and rated the affect of a woman who was either menstruating or who did not provide any menstruating information. The results indicated that there were no significant differences between the two conditions on perceptions of negative affects. The higher a person's ambivalent sexism, the higher the negative perceptions of the woman, regardless of condition. Benevolent Sexism was negatively correlated with the Openness personality trait. Both Benevolent and Hostile Sexism were positively correlated with negative perceptions of the woman's health and affect, regardless of the condition. Agreeableness was positively correlated with positive perceptions of the woman's affect, suggesting that participants higher in Agreeableness were more likely to perceive the woman as having positive emotions, regardless of the condition. We are continuing to collect data to further our research findings.

Affect, Personality, Sexism, and the Menstruating Woman

Emma Jefferson and Po-Sen Chu
Western New Mexico University

Introduction

The stigma that surrounds menstruation can subject women to negative perceptions from others, and significant associations have been found between negative attitudes towards currently menstruating women and hostile sexism (Forbes et al., 2003). Hostile sexism (HS) and benevolent sexism (BS) are damaging types of prejudices. For instance, a study by Lemonaki et al. (2015) indicates that withholding beliefs and displaying behaviors that align with HS can negatively influence a woman's intentions to compete with men. Additionally, both personality and affect seem to be related to people's prevalence of sexism. According to multiple studies, people's certain personality traits are directly correlated to their levels of prejudice, including that of sexism (Ekehammar & Akrami, 2007; Akrami et al., 2011). Also, Marvan et al. (2014) have demonstrated that HS and BS are associated with predictable affect patterns. They found that higher BS is associated with positive yet restricting emotions towards menstruating women, and that higher HS is correlated with negative perceptions of menstruating women. As demonstrated by these studies, it is clear that personality, affect, and negative attitudes are directly associated with ambivalent sexist behavior towards the menstruating woman. Therefore, it is the interest of this study to determine whether ambivalent sexist beliefs and certain personality traits can cause people to perceive women's affect more negatively when menstruation is made salient.

Method

Participants

There were 85 participants recruited from Western New Mexico University's Psychology program. Those who participated received extra credit in their classes. Average age was 27.68 years (SD = 10.69). Sixty-five identified as female, 18 as male, and 1 as other. Most participants identified as White (n = 52).

Measures

Ambivalent Sexism. Ambivalent Sexism was measured using Glick and Fiske's (1996) Ambivalent Sexism Inventory, a 22-item Likert-type scale from 1 = *disagree strongly* to 9 = *agree strongly*. HS and BS were measured by alternating items.

Short Form of Big Five Personality Traits. Personality was measured using a 10-item, Likert-type scale from 1 = *disagree strongly* to 9 = *agree strongly*. Personality traits are Extroversion, Agreeableness, Conscientiousness, Neuroticism, and Openness.

Perception of Woman's Affect and Health. We developed a scale partially based on the Positive and Negative Affect Scale created by Watson et al. (1998). We modified it to assess participants' perception of how the woman is feeling. The Likert-type scale ranged from 1 = *very slightly or not at all* to 9 = *extremely*. The scale contained several filler questions asking about the perceived health of the woman, in order to disguise the purpose of the study. The resulting measures were a Positive Perception of the Woman's Affect (PA), a Negative Perception of the Woman's Affect (NA), a Positive Perception of the Woman's Health (PH), and a Negative Perception of the Woman's Health (NH).

Procedure

Participants completed measures of ambivalent sexism and personality through an online survey created on Google Forms. They were then randomly assigned to one of two groups to view a patient profile and rate the affect of a woman who was either menstruating or who did not provide any menstruating information.

Results

A one-way MANOVA on the PA, NA, PH, and NH variables indicated a non-significant main effect $F(1, 83)$ = 1.33, Wilk's Lambda = 0.94, Eta-squared = 0.06.

The correlations among the scales are presented in Table 1. We conducted zero order correlations and found that the higher the BS, the higher the NA and NH (r = 0.32 and r = 0.24, respectively), and the higher the HS, the higher the NA and NH (0.50 and 0.38, respectively). Therefore, regardless of condition, participants higher in ambivalent sexism perceived the woman to feel more negative emotions and feel more ill.

We also found that BS was negatively correlated with Openness (r = -0.38), so participants higher in benevolent sexism were lower in Openness. Interestingly, Agreeableness was found to be positively correlated with PA (r = 0.30), so participants higher in Agreeableness were more likely to perceive the woman as feeling more positive emotions.

Table 1

Means, Standard Deviations, and Intercorrelations of Measures

Measures	M (SD)	1	2	3	4	5	6	7	8	9	10	11
1. BS	4.20 (1.89)	—										
2. HS	4.10 (1.95)	.43**	—									
3. Extroversion	4.80 (2.10)	-.08	-.02	—								
4. Agreeableness	6.42 (1.77)	.01	.23*	.08	—							
5. Conscientiousness	6.42 (1.87)	.05	.19	.19*	.27*	—						
6. Neuroticism	3.62 (1.90)	.04	.19	-.13	.44**	.13	—					
7. Openness	6.31 (1.68)	-.38**	-.18*	.18	.10	.09	-.28**	—				
8. PA	4.39 (1.95)	.16	.08	.13	.30*	-.04	.20	.11	—			
9. NA	3.21 (1.91)	.32*	.50**	.06	.01	.03	.01	-.02	.05	—		
10. PH	4.86 (1.94)	.11	-.28	.08	.05	-.03	-.13	.02	.44**	.14	—	
11. NH	3.32 (1.45)	.24*	.38**	-.13	.04	-.01	.23	-.08	-.14	.40**	-.21	—

*$p < .05$; **$p < .01$

Discussion

This study examined the relationship between ambivalent sexist beliefs, personality traits, and perception of menstruating women's affect. Although the research hypothesis was not supported, we did find that ambivalent sexism was correlated to negative perception of women's affect. Also, people higher in benevolent sexism were lower in the Openness personality trait.

A significant limitation of this study may be that the information in the menstruation-condition was not made salient enough. In the patient profile for this condition, we listed "Currently menstruating" with the "yes" check-box selected. Participants may have skipped over this information, resulting in no significant difference being found.

Future research could also benefit from using three conditions: one in which the woman is menstruating, one in which the woman is not menstruating, and one in which no menstruation information is given.

Additionally, participants were primarily female and White college students recruited from Psychology classes. So, future research may benefit from ensuring other gender-identities and people of color are more accurately represented within the sample.

Our findings could potentially contribute to the further understanding of ambivalent sexism and its relationship with people's general perceptions of women.

Selected References

Akrami, N., Ekehammar, B., & Yang-Wallentin, F. (2011). Personality and Social Psychology Factors Explaining Sexism. *Journal of Individual Differences, 32*(3), 154 -160. 10.1027/1614-0001/a000043

Ekehammar, B., & Akrami, N. (2007). Personality and Prejudice: From Big Five Personality Factors to Facets. *Journal of Personality, 75*(3), 899-926. 10.1111/j.1467 -6494.2007.00460.x

Forbes, G. B., Adams-Curtis, L. E., White, K. B., Holmgren, K. M. (2003). The role of hostile and benevolent sexism in women's and men's perceptions of the menstruating woman. *Psychology of Women Quarterly 27*(1), 58-63. 2003/01.1111/1471-6402.t01-2-00007

Lemonaki, E, Manstead, A. S. R., Maio, G. R. (2015). Hostile sexism (de)motivates women's social competition intentions: The contradictory role of emotions. *Journal of Social Psychology, 54*, 483-499. 10.1111/bjso.12100

Marvan, M. L., Vacio-Tobeda, R., Christie, J. C., (2014). Ambivalent sexism, attitudes towards menstruation and menstrual cycle-related symptoms. *International Journal of Psychology, 49*(4), 280-287. 10.1002/ijop.12003

Watson, D, Clark, L. A., Tellegen, A. (1998). Development and validation of brief measures of positive and negative affect: the PANAS scales. *Journal of Personality and Social Psychology, 54*(6), 1063-1070. 10.1037/0022-3514.54.6.1063

Correspondence may be sent to:
Emma Jefferson (ejefferson@wnmu.edu)
Dr. Po-Sen Chu (chup@wnmu.edu)

Foliar Effects of Nano vs. Bulk Materials on Kidney Bean Plants

SIDNEY QUEZADA

Foliar Effects of Nano vs. Bulk Materials on Kidney Bean Plants

Sidney Quezada; Chala Werber; Goyce Koeppl; Illya Medina-Velo

Western New Mexico University

Abstract

- This experiment evaluates the effect of foliar application of silicon, zinc, and manganese compounds to fight drought stress in kidney bean plants.
- It examines the efficiency of bulk (1000 micrometers) versus nanomaterial (1-100 nanometers) commercial compounds.

Introduction

Silicon (Si), zinc (Zn), and manganese (Mn) are essential plant nutrients used on crops to aid plants in growth[1,2,3], to fight drought stress[2], and develop pathogen resistance[1].

Since the particle size of agrochemicals plays an integral role in the uptake and distribution in plants due to changes in the physical and chemical properties[5,6].

It has been proposed to use nanomaterials in agriculture to enhance fertilizer efficiency[7].

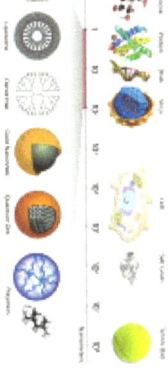

Methods

1. Seed Germination

Natural soil was mixed with Happy Frog Soil Conditioner (3:1). 5 kidney bean seeds were properly washed and planted in the soil mixture. 0.584 grams of salt was dissolved in 100 ml of water and given to plants. Pots were placed under growth lights with a 12-hour photoperiod.

2. Treatments

Two weeks after germination, suspensions of 60 ppm of Zn, 300 ppm of Si, and 75 ppm of Mn bulk and nano-size were prepared and sprayed on leaves of bean plants 24 times once at the beginning of the experiment.

3. Harvest

Plant height and chlorophyll levels were measured, and a sample of soil was collected for analysis.

Samples of stems, roots, leaves, and soil were collected. Fresh weight was recorded.

For future analysis, one set of leaves, stems, and roots from each plant were stored at a -80°C.

The rest of the samples were placed in an oven at 80°C for 72h. Then dry weight was recorded.

4. Analysis

Dry samples were ground down with a mortar and pestle for elemental analysis of all the tissues. Frozen samples will be used for enzyme analysis.

Results and Discussion

- Chlorophyll levels were significantly reduced by nano-Zn and Mn and all bulk compounds.

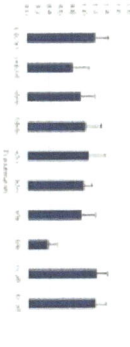

- Both bulk and nano treatments had a positive effect on fresh weight of stems, leaves and roots. Although not significant in all cases.
- Seed fresh weight was not significantly affected by any treatment.
- The combination of Mn, Zn, and Si did not benefit the plant growth compared to some individual treatments

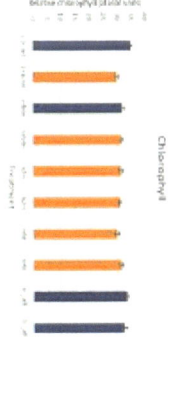

Literature Cited

1. Ma, J. F. (2004). Role of silicon in enhancing the resistance of plants to biotic and abiotic stresses. Soil science and plant nutrition, 50(1), 11-18.
2. Hassan, M. U., Aamer, M., Cathia, M. U., Haiying T., Shazad B., Barbanti, L., Nawaz, M., Rasheed, A., Afzal, A., Liu, Y., Guoquin, H. (2020). The Critical Role of Zinc in Plants Facing the Drought Stress. Agriculture, 10(9), 1-20.
3. Hafeez, B., Khanif, Y.M., Saleem, M. (2013). Role of Zinc in Plant Nutrition- A Review. Journal of Experimental Agriculture International, 3(2), 374-391.
4. Schmidt, S.D., Husted, S. (2019) The Biochemical Properties of Manganese in Plants. Plants, 8(10), 381.
5. Rawle, A. (2002). The Importance of particle size to the coating industry Part: 1 Particle size measurement. Advances in Colour Science and Technology, 5(1), 1-12.
6. Judy, J.B., Unrine J.M., Rao, W., Wirick, S., Bertsch P.M. (2012) Bioavailability of Gold Nanomaterials to Plants: Importance of Particle Size and Surface Coating Environmental Science and Technology 46(15), 8467-8474.
7. Guo, H., White, J.C., Wang, Z.,King, B. (2018) Nano-enabled fertilizers to control the release and efficiency of nutrients. Current Opinion in Environmental Science & Health, 6, 77-83.

Acknowledgements:
- NM-AMP
- The United States Department of Agriculture and The National Institute of Food and Agriculture [award number 2020-70001-31287]

www.ingramcontent.com/pod-product-compliance
Lightning Source LLC
Chambersburg PA
CBHW041616120626

46551CB00003B/469